**YALE LECTURES ON THE
RESPONSIBILITIES OF CITIZENSHIP**

THE RELATIONS BETWEEN

FREEDOM AND RESPONSIBILITY

IN THE EVOLUTION OF DEMOCRATIC
GOVERNMENT

IN THE SAME SERIES.

THE RELATION BETWEEN FREEDOM AND RESPONSIBILITY IN THE EVOLUTION OF DEMOCRATIC GOVERNMENT. By ARTHUR T. HADLEY, President of Yale University. 12mo. $1.00 *net*.

THE CITIZEN IN HIS RELATION TO THE INDUSTRIAL SITUATION. By HENRY C. POTTER, D.D., LL.D., Bishop of New York. 12mo. $1.00 *net*.

AMERICAN CITIZENSHIP. By DAVID J. BREWER, Associate Justice, Supreme Court of the United States. 12mo. 75 cents *net*.

THE RELATIONS BETWEEN
FREEDOM
AND
RESPONSIBILITY
IN THE EVOLUTION
OF DEMOCRATIC GOVERNMENT

BY

ARTHUR TWINING HADLEY

PRESIDENT OF YALE UNIVERSITY

AUTHOR OF "ECONOMICS," "RAILROAD TRANSPORTATION,"
"THE EDUCATION OF THE AMERICAN CITIZEN"

NEW YORK
CHARLES SCRIBNER'S SONS
1903

COPYRIGHT, 1903

BY YALE UNIVERSITY

Published, December, 1903

TROW DIRECTORY
PRINTING AND BOOKBINDING COMPANY
NEW YORK

TO

THE MEMORY OF

WILLIAM EARL DODGE

FOUNDER OF THE YALE LECTURES ON THE

RESPONSIBILITIES OF CITIZENSHIP

WHO HIMSELF ACCEPTED THOSE RESPONSIBILITIES

IN THE FULLEST MEASURE

AND WHO

BY HIS CHARACTER AND HIS EXAMPLE

INSPIRED OTHERS TO

DO LIKEWISE

PREFACE

FOR the successful conduct of a nation's affairs, we must have a certain degree of conformity between its political institutions and the moral character of its members. There is one set of virtues which fits men to be subjects of a monarchy; there is another very different set which is requisite for the citizens of a free commonwealth.

We find a tendency among many people at the present day to claim the political rights of free citizens without accepting the moral obligations which go with them. But the attempt to assume the privileges of freedom and disclaim its responsibilities is fatal to the nation which tolerates it; and theories of law or schemes of social reform which ignore this ethical basis of democracy are likely to prove suicidal.

It is the object of this book to show what this ethical basis of democracy is, how it has arisen, and what happens if we try to ignore it.

CONTENTS

		PAGE
I.	Democracy in Theory and in Practice	1
II.	The Basis of Civil Liberty	26
III.	Freedom as a Religious Conception	48
IV.	Freedom as a Legal Institution	73
V.	Freedom as a Foundation of Ethics	102
VI.	The Limits of Individual Freedom	126
VII.	The Outlook for the Future	150

FREEDOM AND RESPONSIBILITY

I

DEMOCRACY IN THEORY AND IN PRACTICE

THE ordinary student of public affairs is content to classify governments by their external form. He calls them monarchies, aristocracies, or democracies, according as the supreme authority rests in the hands of an individual, a privileged class, or a large body of citizens; and having thus labelled a political society with one of these three names, he thinks that he knows something about its real character.

But the man who goes more deeply into the subject sees that the form of government is an unimportant thing as compared with the spirit in which government is administered. A king or a privileged class ruling in accordance with traditions and trying to act for the interests of the people will give a much larger measure of real freedom than is possible under a democracy whose members have no respect for the past and no higher aim than their own selfish advancement. In 1793 France was a democracy, England an aristocracy; but the actual amount of liberty enjoyed in England was decidedly greater than in France. The more a man knows of political history, the more he will appreciate the reasons which led Aristotle to divide all governments into two fundamentally distinct classes: the legitimate and the illegitimate. Legitimate governments are administered in the interest of the whole body politic, under a system of traditions whose gradual growth and preservation is the best guarantee that this public interest is subserved. Illegitimate governments are administered in the interest of the governing body—be it an individual, a small group, or a large number of free citizens—with relatively little regard for the wider interests of the body politic, and without any adequate restraints of tradition. This internal character or spirit of a government is far more important than any of its external characteristics. With unselfish purpose and adherence to tradition any government, whatever its form, may be said to exist by the consent of the governed. Without such unselfish purpose and adherence to tradition, monarchy degenerates into tyranny, aristocracy into oligarchy, democracy into populism.

As far as monarchy and aristocracy are concerned, these dangers are sufficiently obvious. It is easy to see that a monarch, acting for his own selfish ends, may declare himself independent of the law and become a tyrant. It is easy to see that an aristocracy, preferring class interest to public interest, may degenerate into the rule of an element which is far from being the best in the state. It is plain enough that a king or a nobleman does not deserve to continue in office unless he regards political power as a trust to be exercised in behalf of society as a whole. But it has not always been recognized that the same dangers exist in a democracy, and that a democratic people needs to be animated by the same sense of trusteeship in the exercise of its political functions.

Some men believe that the mere existence of democracy renders it impossible that public affairs should be administered in the interests of a class or group. They think that government by popular election will necessarily mean government for the people. They hold that if a state, nominally democratic, is managed for the benefit of a favored few, it simply proves that the elections are being improperly conducted—in other words, that we have before us not a democracy, but an oligarchy masquerading under a false name. Men who look at things in this way have urged an equalization of political power among all classes as a sovereign remedy for public ills. Others, who do not go to this extreme and are clear-headed enough to admit the possibility of abuse of democratic authority, nevertheless believe that with a proper legal machinery of checks and balances the dangers of this abuse can be reduced to a minimum and perhaps altogether avoided. They think that a constitution can be framed in such a way that the people can let their political life be governed by considerations of self-interest without serious detriment—nay, perhaps with positive advantage—to the necessities of the republic as a whole.

Each of these views is erroneous, and may readily become dangerous. The error in the second is less obvious than in the first; but the practical dangers which arise from its prevalence are all the greater on that account. It is probably quite as necessary for the citizens of a democratic state to regard political power as a public trust, to be exercised for the benefit of others, as it is for a monarch or an aristocrat. The acceptance of this responsibility and trusteeship goes with the successful exercise of every kind of freedom—moral, social, or civil. Any attempt to claim freedom and disclaim responsibility, under whatever name or form of government, proves illusory or self-destructive.

The danger of relying on unrestricted democracy

was most clearly illustrated at the time of the French Revolution of 1789. The leaders of that movement, when they swept away the evils which had been incident to an outworn system of class privileges, thought that it would be sufficient for them to give equality of voting power in order to have the government administered in the general interest. They were so enamored of Rousseau's phrases about the sovereignty of the people that they neglected his warnings against short cuts toward the exercise of that sovereignty. The consequences which followed are only too well known. Whoever at any given moment commanded the majority of votes in the National Assembly deemed himself, for the time being, the exponent of the public will, and regarded his personal judgment as the index of public opinion. Each believed that he was the accredited agent of the whole people. At the end of the seventeenth century Louis XIV had said, "I am the State." With equal fervor of conviction Marat, or Danton, or Robespierre was ready to pronounce those same words at the end of the eighteenth. Louis XIV, in spite of his absolute political authority, was subject to some restraints of custom and tradition. The revolutionary leaders recognized no such restraints, and were for that reason even more liable to abuse their power.

That their government in theory represented the will of the whole people only made matters worse in practice, because it removed moral restraints which would otherwise have made themselves felt. The fact that Danton regarded himself as the community's representative was the very thing which rendered him most unsafe to the community. It has been said that virtue is more dangerous than vice, because its excesses are not subject to the restraints of conscience. It was these excesses of supposed virtue which made the Reign of Terror possible. The men who, like St. Just, were most irreproachable in their private character, were the very ones to be most unscrupulous in the use of judicial murder for what they supposed to be the public interest.

It is easy to point out the fallacy in the views of the French Revolutionary leaders. They did not properly distinguish between the government and the people. They supposed that when the people elected the government, the members of that government became, *ipso facto*, the mouthpieces of the popular will. This of course did not follow. A person who was elected to office might be a bad man, whose wishes would be as tyrannical as those of the most degraded monarch. Or he might be a misguided man, who would mistake his own false judgments for the opinion of the people as a whole.

DEMOCRACY IN THEORY AND PRACTICE 7

Or—and this is perhaps the hardest thing of all to avoid—even if he were honest and clear-headed, and tried to carry out the wishes of the majority who had elected him, this majority might have interests of its own which it would use for the detriment and the oppression of the minority. In none of these cases would the government really represent the interests of the body politic. The more unchecked the power of a political leader under any of these circumstances, the greater was the probability of oppression and of class legislation.

The failure of the French to appreciate this distinction between the people and their elective officials was largely due to the fact that democratic power was given to them too suddenly. They had had no chance to experiment with its exercise in detail, and could hardly fail to be misled by false theories when they were suddenly called upon to apply it on a large scale. In England and in the English colonies of America, where the growth of freedom was more gradual, the chance for experiments in self-government had been larger, and the danger from false theories was correspondingly less. So long as our ancestors were stating principles, they stated them very much as the French did. But when they set out to apply them to the actual work of government, they took pains to avoid the practical difficulties of which they had already had experience. The Declaration of Independence contains theories closely resembling those of Rousseau; but the Constitution of the United States is as different from any of the French constitutions at the close of the eighteenth century as a practical machine is different from a whirligig. The English and American liberals relied on restricted or constitutional democracy as a means of avoiding the evils which had sprung from monarchy or aristocracy on the one hand, and from unrestrained popular power on the other. The framers of our Constitution set out with a definite problem before them—the problem of constructing a working government which should give effect to the will of the people and at the same time provide efficient safeguards for individual liberty. When their theories seemed likely to secure this result, they stated them boldly. When they seemed likely to interfere with it, they quietly ignored them.

The main points which our ancestors had thus learned from the history of the English Parliament and from their own experience in the colonial assemblies may be summed up in a few words.

A representative assembly or convention, composed of delegates from different sections of the community, had its chief usefulness as a forum for discussion and a means of forming public opinion. For this purpose it was admirably adapted. For conducting the real business of government it was not well fitted. If it attempted to perform this work itself it was vacillating in policy, and arbitrary and irresolute by turns. This had been exemplified in the sessions of the Continental Congress. It had been almost equally conspicuous in England during the struggle between the King and Parliament in the middle of the seventeenth century. There are times when firmness of purpose and promptitude of action, even though it be somewhat unwise, are preferable to the wisest deliberation protracted to an undue length. Armies, says Macaulay, have won victories under bad generals, but no army ever won a victory under a debating society. If, on the other hand, the convention or parliament recognized these limitations, and did not attempt to perform the actual work of administration, but found within its ranks some leader to whom it was ready to delegate its powers, that leader soon became strong enough to reduce the assembly to a mere cipher and to exercise an authority none the less despotic because decently veiled under some of the forms of popular government. This had been England's experience in the case of Cromwell; and it is one which, on a larger or smaller scale, almost every democratic nation has been forced to repeat.

To meet these dangers, the American Constitution provided that the actual work of government should not be performed either by the legislative assembly, or by an appointee of that assembly, but by an officer chosen through another body called the electoral college. It was to be the duty of this college to deliberate on the choice of president and vice-president; and, having performed that duty, to terminate its official life, leaving the president free to act in the sphere of government assigned him, while the legislature, within its own sphere, still possessed its full force and had not abrogated or delegated any of its powers. These powers of the legislature, or Congress, under the American Constitution, were similar to those which were actually exercised at the time by the English Parliament. It could pass laws after proper debate, and it could exercise indirect control over the acts of the executive by its power of withholding supplies, and by certain other means which the Constitution provided in order to prevent the president from arbitrarily disregarding the wishes of the people as expressed in Congress. It was further provided that the executive authority of the president and the legislative authority of Congress were to be

DEMOCRACY IN THEORY AND PRACTICE 11

exercised only within definite limits and under restrictions set by custom or rendered advisable by experience. Some of these were incorporated in the Constitution; others were involved in the tacit acceptance of English legal principles. Courts were established, whose members were appointed by the executive but whose tenure of office rendered them independent of arbitrary whims of that executive, which could define the application of these principles and prevent the President or the Congress from transgressing them.

This is a picture, necessarily brief and imperfect, but fair in its essential outlines, of the most important attempt which the world has seen to provide machinery of democratic self-government. It indicates the dangers which the framers of our Constitution anticipated and the methods which they actually employed to meet them. In the light of a full century of experience, what shall we say of their success?

In the main, they succeeded well. The specific things which they set out to do they unquestionably brought about. They established a government sufficiently popular to prevent revolution, and yet sufficiently conservative to secure prosperity. There have been no dangerous acts of usurpation on the part of the executive. This branch of the government has been always fairly strong, and in emergencies exceedingly strong, without in general becoming arbitrary or oppressive. There has been an independent activity of President, Congress and courts which has, to some degree, followed the lines which Hamilton and Madison had in mind. The safeguards of traditional usage have been maintained; and the courts have exercised a control over arbitrary acts of the legislature, at once more extended and more salutary than was deemed possible at the outset.

To a certain extent, then, the framers of the Constitution may be said to have protected us against the dangers of assumption of arbitrary power in the interests of an individual or a class. But this is true only to a certain extent. In providing against one set of dangers which they could anticipate from past experience they exposed us to another set which they could not thus anticipate.

It was, I think, the tacit assumption of the members of the Constitutional Convention that the various representative bodies which it provided—the electoral college and the two houses of Congress—would be organs for the formation of public opinion. Coming from different parts of the country, their members would enlighten one another as to the views and needs of American citizens in different places, and would thus be able to arrive at a common understanding concerning the views and needs of the nation as a whole, which they in turn would report to their constituents and defend against local criticism. This had been the essential character of the English Parliament down to the close of the eighteenth century. It was, as its name implied, a *parliament*—a place for debating. By its debates it held up to public odium the tyrannical acts of the king which otherwise might have escaped notice, and created a common public sentiment which made all parts of the kingdom ready to resist infringement on the liberties of any. In the earlier days of Parliament, all its other achievements and powers were small in comparison with this. But during the course of the nineteenth century these debating functions of the English Parliament, and of other representative bodies modelled upon it, became much less important. The post office, the newspaper, the telegraph, caused public opinion to be formed in advance, before any representative assembly could meet. As soon as this change took place, the importance of parliamentary discussion almost necessarily died away. The electoral college had been originally intended as a body for debate, whose members should make up their minds, after consultation, as to the candidate whose election would best subserve the interests of the whole body politic; but it soon became a mere machine for registering instructions previously given to its members by the convention of the party which elected them. A similar result has made itself felt in the houses of Congress; more slowly and less completely, indeed, because it is impossible for a convention to instruct its representatives as explicitly on the various points of legislation which are likely to arise as it can instruct them on the ballot to be cast for a president or a vice-president, but none the less inevitably. Congressional debate, which by one generation of our statesmen was used as a means of forming public opinion, became in the second generation only a means of expressing or justifying the attitude of a section, and in the third generation is barely tolerated as a survival of ancient practices, to be cut short whenever the exigencies of business demand it. For, coincident with this decline in the demand for debate, there has been an increase in the amount of business to be done. A thousand details occupy the attention of each branch of our legislature for one that might have come before it a century ago. With so little time for public discussion, and so many practical measures to be pushed through, it is not surprising that the average congressman of today has ceased to regard it as his

DEMOCRACY IN THEORY AND PRACTICE 15

primary duty to shape public opinion by his utterances, his votes, and his personal influence. On questions of party policy he deems himself commissioned to register the will of those who elected him, and on all non-partisan matters to use his utmost efforts to despatch such business as the interests of his district most urgently demand.

In an assembly of this kind the work of government tends to degenerate into a series of attempts to promote partisan or local interests, rather than to unite all persons in the pursuit of a common interest. Even when legislators honestly strive to resist this tendency, they are often powerless to overcome it. The efforts of the leaders are, and of necessity must be, directed toward the securing of a majority, rather than toward the convincing of a minority. The acts of a body under such leadership are a series of negotiations rather than discussions, looking toward compromise rather than toward mutual enlightenment. It is urged by those who defend the system that these negotiations and these struggles are conducted on fair terms; that the local and partisan efforts of some men in certain directions are balanced by the equally free efforts of other men in other directions; that a majority which abuses its powers will soon find itself in a minority; and that, in short, the free play of this conflict of parties and districts gives quite as equitable results as any other system which has been devised. We have hardly time to stop and consider how far these views are justified. Whatever may be said in extenuation of the evils, it frequently happens in the work of modern legislative assemblies that the fair claims of minorities are ruthlessly sacrificed; that those who would defend the public treasury from the effects of extravagant appropriation bills are overborne by a coalition of those who see in a group of such bills a special advantage to the interests which they represent; and that the interests of those so organized that they can at the moment command many votes are allowed to outweigh far weightier interests which are not so circumstanced. Whatever may be the final outcome of the struggle, the immediate effort of the leaders of our representative assemblies works toward what Aristotle calls illegitimate government—government by a group in its own interest, rather than in the interest of the whole body politic.

This effect is not peculiar to the United States. It has been felt to a greater or less degree in England, in France, and in Germany. But there is one special set of conditions in the American Constitution which has made the change go farther in the United States than anywhere else, and has rendered the resulting problems very much more difficult to meet.

The framers of our Constitution, in order to avoid the danger of usurpation by the president, reduced to a minimum the connection between the executive and legislative departments of the government; and at the same time they so arranged the powers of each of these departments that neither could be very effective without the other. The legislative work of Congress was subject to the president's veto. The executive work of the president was dependent for its effective prosecution upon the good-will of a congressional, and especially of a senatorial, majority. Each department had it in its power to thwart the efforts of the other. This was a good thing in extreme cases, when either department wished to violate the Constitution; but in ordinary cases, when we wanted to have the regular work of government smoothly and effectively performed, it was always inconvenient and sometimes bad. No private corporation can be efficiently managed when it is run by two independent sets of authorities at the same time. What is true of a private corporation is equally true of a public corporation. Division of authority causes work to be done slowly, and prevents people from fixing the responsibility for its failure or inefficiency. In England, where the prime minister, representing a Parliamentary majority, constitutes the real executive, we know fairly well where to award the praise or blame for what is going on. If Parliament passes the bills which he desires, the prime minister takes the responsibility. If Parliament will not pass the bills which he desires, he withdraws from office and leaves some one else to do better if he can. But in the United States we have a president, representing the people in one way, and Congress, representing the people in another way. If the two powers are at issue each blames the other.

It will occasionally happen that the president can dominate Congress by his ability, as did Washington or Lincoln. It will perhaps somewhat more frequently happen that he can manage it by his tact, as did McKinley. But unless he possesses exceptional power in one of these directions, some special agency is needed for coördinating the work of the two parts of the government which the American Constitution has not only left independent, but has tried to force into a degree of independence that is quite unnatural.

This agency is found in the party machinery.

If any business needs to be done which requires the coöperation of both the executive and legislative departments of the government, a quick way to get

DEMOCRACY IN THEORY AND PRACTICE 19

at it—and often the only way to get at it—is to see that it is approved in the regular channels of party organization. If it secures this approval, all goes smoothly. If it does not secure this approval, it is blocked in all manner of unexpected ways. That this state of things exists is quite generally recognized. That it is a price we pay for the benefits enjoyed under the Constitution of the United States is not, I think, equally well recognized.

I do not, of course, mean that our constitutional provisions are the cause for the existence of parties. Political parties are formed in every legislative assembly, among men of all races and all forms of executive authority. Wherever one group of people wants one set of measures carried, and another group prefers another set, each will organize itself in order to give effect and coherence to its views. To any such organization a certain amount of party machinery is incident. But where there is a lack of proper connection between the executive and the legislature, as there was in England in the eighteenth century, or as there is in America under the Constitution today, we find party organization taking a peculiar character. We see parties primarily arranged, not to promote certain measures of legislation, but to do the work of government. The party machine as an administrative body becomes the main thing; the legislative measures with which it is identified are only an incident. I believe this to have been the usual condition in the United States, especially in later years. Occasionally we find exceptions. The democratic party in the generation preceding the war was influenced by men who cared for state sovereignty as against centralization, and were willing to sacrifice office rather than compromise this principle. The republican party from 1856 to 1870 was dominated by men who cared more for free soil and for the Union than they did for their own positions of authority or political power. But these are hardly the normal types of American party life. Under ordinary circumstances the work of persuading the executive and legislature to work in harmony under the somewhat strained conditions presented by the United States Constitution seems more important than the passing of any particular measures; and that side of the party organization naturally and inevitably comes to the front.

This method of government, whatever merits it may have, is obviously not government by the people and for the people. It is government by a particular section of the people; and, primarily at any rate, for the interests of that section. If the voters who form a certain party are men of liberal ideas and just principles, their leaders will of course not go so far to oppress the minority as they would if their constituents were narrow-minded and reckless of moral restraint. But even at best partisan majorities are quite inconsiderate of minority interests. I suppose all men, independent of their traditional affiliations, can now see that the democrats in the years immediately preceding the war, and the republicans in the years immediately following the war, were both rather unscrupulous in the use of the machinery of government to promote the interests of the sections which they chiefly represented. A party, as its very name implies, represents a part, and not the whole. The fact that it has no recognized status in the Constitution makes it all the more difficult to fix public responsibilities upon its real leaders, because they do their work without official recognition, and therefore without the acceptance of those duties which such recognition usually brings.

There is no need of citing detailed instances of wrong and oppression which come through the machinery of party government, or of the temptations to corruption which the existence of such machinery furnishes. We find quite enough of this set forth at length in the columns of any newspaper opposed to the dominant authority. I conceive that there can be no doubt on the main propositions that parties are organized for the interests of a section of the community rather than for the whole; that they have developed in a way not intended or expected by the framers of the Constitution; that these organizations, representing class interests, are things which it is extremely difficult to hold responsible, legally or morally, in the way that a recognized public official could be held responsible; and that for the sake of carrying an election they may commit themselves to measures which are likely to do great damage, not only to the minority but to the interests of the community as a whole. In other words, the separation of the legislative and executive branches of the government has offered no adequate safeguard against the tyranny of the majority over the minority. The Reconstruction Acts furnished a visible instance of such tyranny, from which we have by no means recovered. The corporation laws of certain states in the years following the crisis of 1873 furnished another conspicuous instance. Even in recent years there has been more than one campaign fought out on an issue of class interests, in which our escape from serious legislative dangers has been very narrow indeed.

Nor is it in Congress alone that we suffer from this tyranny of the majority through the medium of party organization. The increasing centraliza tion of all authority, industrial as well as political, and the increased activity of communication between different parts of the body politic have caused boards of councilmen or state legislatures to handle matters which were formerly left to the individual, and national authorities to deal with many problems which were formerly entrusted to local ones. The rule that every man should mind his own business is not so easy to follow as it once was; and when a legislator is forced to mind other people's business, there is a great temptation to sacrifice interests which command only a few votes to those which command a great many.

Neither in nation, nor in state, nor in city, have these dangers of government interference been to any appreciable degree avoided by the separation of executive and legislative powers. For protection against them we rely upon the courts. The work of the courts in this respect, taking it as a whole, has been extremely salutary. There have indeed been times when the suspicion of partisanship has attached to American judicial utterances; but they have been singularly few. On the whole, federal and state courts alike have been not only a protection, but the one really efficient protection, of minority interests against oppression by the majority. Our constitutional rights against deprivation of personal liberty, against the taking of property without due process of law, and against the infringement of contractual obligations—not to speak of others less habitually called in question—have been defined and administered by the courts with a rare degree of success. It has more than once happened that an impatient majority has denounced these courts as instruments of partisanship. The anti-slavery leaders, the soft money leaders, and the labor leaders, have in turn taken exception to their utterances, and even ventured to impugn their motives. But I think that most intelligent men who know the history of the country will say that our courts have been the real bulwarks of American liberty; and that while Hamilton and his associates would be somewhat disappointed in the working of the machinery of legislation and administration if they could see it in its present shape, they would be filled with admiration at the work which has been accomplished by the judiciary. I believe it to be the judgment of sober-minded men that the courts have furnished the agency which has guarded us against partisan excesses, and have saved the American republic from the necessity of repeating the successive revolutionary experiences which France underwent before she could attain to a stable democracy.

And yet this department of our government, which has thus been essential to the preservation of liberty, is precisely the one which represents *restraint*. This is the distinctive function exercised by the courts. Legislature and executive are means given to allow the people to do what they please, under certain constitutional forms. The judiciary is a means given to prevent the people from doing what they please. How can we explain the fact that these judicial restrictions are of the very essence of freedom? I answer, because the law of the United States, as defined and administered by its courts, represents not only restraint, but *self*-restraint; and a kind of self-restraint which any nation must be prepared to exercise, if it hopes permanently to enjoy the advantages of political freedom.

II

THE BASIS OF CIVIL LIBERTY

We saw in the previous chapter that a democracy, however well organized, is liable to degenerate into government by a section of the people, administered primarily to suit the views and interests of that section; in other words, that the danger of the tyranny of a majority is no less real than the danger of the tyranny of a monarch or a ruling class. We saw also that the machinery of the American Constitution, which was intended to reduce this danger by the separation of legislative and executive power, had in some ways actually increased it, by the need which it created for strong party organizations to assist in the work of government; and that for a really effective check upon the partisan attempts of the majority to abridge the freedom of the minority we had come to rely on the action of the courts.

But what gives the courts this power? What is it that enables them to say to majorities, "Thus far shalt thou go, and no farther"? By what right do they stand as an effective bar to president or congress, to governor or general assembly?

THE BASIS OF CIVIL LIBERTY 27

Most people would reply: "They derive the power from the Constitution of the United States itself." To some extent this answer is a true one. The Constitution specifically provides against certain abuses of authority on the part of the executive or the legislature. No person may be deprived of property without due process of law. The courts are naturally the authorities to determine what constitutes a person and what is due process of law. No state may pass any statute impairing the obligation of contracts. The courts are at hand to say what constitutes an obligation of contract, and are directly charged with the duty of preventing its impairment. In any case arising under either of these heads—and a very large number of pieces of class legislation are included under the one or the other—the Constitution furnishes the clearest evidence that the court has the right and duty to interfere. The court can therefore rest its authority on that document; and it is extremely convenient for it to do so, because the great majority of the people loyally accept the Constitution, even when its results work adversely to their own interests.

But it would, I think, be idle to pretend that the Constitution was the *cause* of judicial authority and of public self-restraint. The Constitution does not cause self-restraint to be practised; self-restraint causes the Constitution to be obeyed. In the absence of such voluntary self-restraint, constitutional provisions would be a singularly ineffective bar against aggression. If people whose interests are adversely affected by our constitutional limitations should choose to organize for the purpose of bettering their legal position, they would often find themselves numerous enough to secure the necessary amendments. It is not in itself a very difficult thing to get a change made in the United States Constitution. Those parts of that instrument which deal with our political machinery have been repeatedly amended. But it is a significant and interesting fact that those parts which deal with private rights have not been altered, except in the single case of the Fourteenth Amendment; and this alteration was largely unintentional, for the effect of the Fourteenth Amendment in increasing the immunity of corporations from adverse legislation was not contemplated at the time of its passage. People have shrunk from modifying a public document to suit their own private interests.

Nor have the federal courts limited their activity to those points where the Constitution provided a specific warrant for its exercise. They have applied the traditional restraints and the traditional methods of interpretation familiar to the law of

England in such a way as to limit the power of the legislature, even where a statute did not come into direct conflict with constitutional provisions. What has been true of the federal courts has been equally true of the state courts. No small part of the judicial protection of minorities against the abuse of the power of the majority has been accomplished by means other than those directly prescribed in the United States Constitution, and on grounds of which that instrument takes no cognizance.

If we pass from the United States to England, where there is no document corresponding to the Constitution of the United States, but where the habits of legal procedure and public activity closely resemble our own, we shall find the courts exercising a similar power in protecting the rights of the individual. This power has not the same theoretical warrant for its exercise which exists in America. The English theory is that Parliament is legally omnipotent; and the existence of such a theory causes no small anxiety to some of the conservative interests in England at the present day. But the English habit and practice is to insist rigidly on all customary rights, whatever Parliament may say about them; and the effect of this usage in limiting the power of legislation makes England far freer than those countries which have more explicitly defined constitutional limitations but less habit of exercising individual independence in the face of a clamorous majority.

A written constitution serves much the same purpose in public law which a fence serves in the definition and protection of private rights to real estate. A fence does not make a boundary; it marks one. If it is set where a boundary line has previously existed by tradition and agreement, it forms an exceedingly convenient means of defending it against encroachments. If it is set near the boundary and allowed to stay there unchallenged, it may in time become itself the accepted boundary. But if the attempt is made to establish a factitious boundary by the mere act of setting up a fence, the effort fails. In like manner, a constitution which simply defines the powers and limitations of governmental authority furnishes an excellent means of defending private rights against usurpation; and the provisions of such a constitution may cause rights to become definite and defensible which previously were uncertain or inoperative. But a mere paper constitution, established without reference to previous usages and habits, is not effective in creating a new scheme of political and social order. The constitution is the evidence of a limitation, not its cause.

THE BASIS OF CIVIL LIBERTY

The real limitation to the unbridled power of majorities is to be found in the habit of the American people of governing themselves by tradition and reason. Not that this habit is confined to the Americans. It is equally exemplified among the English. It is possessed, in greater or less measure, by every nation which has succeeded in solving problems of self-government. In order that men may live peacefully and do business successfully it is necessary that their dealings with one another should be marked by a high degree of continuity and a fair measure of good sense. These are the assumptions on which civilized society rests. The courts enable people to carry this way of doing things into difficult cases where reason is blinded by selfishness, and where possession of political power tempts men to depart from tradition. The American judiciary is the part of the United States government which bases its authority upon the assumption that people wish to be rational and conservative. A judicial decision does not, like a statute, merely say what things must be done; it states both precedents and reasons which show why those things must be done. Sometimes, indeed, these decisions seem to be too much based on precedent alone, and too little on reason. They seem to the more radical members of the community to preserve vested rights at the expense of public interests. But this is the safe side on which to err. Burke, in his Reflections on the French Revolution, has well expressed one main reason for the permanence and success of the government of England, when he says that Englishmen are afraid to cut loose from prejudice and rely on individual reason because they suspect that in each man the stock of reason is small, and prefer to avail themselves of the bank and capital of ages.

A judicial decision differs from other edicts of the government in that it does not involve an arbitrary expression of will. It puts the reasons for the prescribed course of conduct in such a form as to command general consent, first among the experts learned in the law, and next among the great body of people who are not learned in the law, but who have the habit of controlling themselves according to custom and precedent. It may occasionally happen that a legal question arises on which no such general consensus is possible. In those cases there will be some vacillation in the decisions of the court. This is always unfortunate; and most of the difficulties which menace judicial authority arise in connection with cases of this kind. Statutes regarding corporations, or labor, or colonial possessions, often deal with conditions which are so far

THE BASIS OF CIVIL LIBERTY

novel that it is not clear which legal precedents most directly apply, or what relative weight should be given to tradition on the one hand and independent judgment on the other. But these points of doubt are exceptional as compared with that large *corpus juris* which is so well settled that people accept it as an inevitable part of the conditions of life, even when it happens to work against their own private interests.

The more broadly we study the history of the law, the more we are impressed with this essentially rational character of public submission to judicial authority. Decisions furnish precedents, and precedents secure unquestioned acquiescence, because the reason which dictated the first decision still holds good with those who examine the matter impartially in subsequent instances. The Prætorian edict at Rome had at first no binding force on any one, except possibly the single magistrate by whom it was issued. But as time went on successive prætors found it expedient and necessary to follow the reasons which governed their predecessors, until there grew up a mass of equity jurisprudence none the less authoritative because of the somewhat informal manner in which it had originated. There is no lack of more recent examples of the same kind. In some of the state appellate courts, notably that of Illinois, it is provided by statute that the decisions of the judges shall furnish no precedent for the action of their successors. But the judges publish reasons for their awards; and these reasons continue to hold good until conditions have changed or until some flaw in their logic can be found. The very act which deprives these courts of the right to create precedents serves only to show more clearly the real nature of the authority which gives precedent its force—the authority which reason exercises upon civilized man.

There is a theory of judicial authority which seems to conflict with this—a theory that law depends for its force, not upon reason, but upon the command of a sovereign. I do not like this way of stating the ground of legal authority, because it is liable to be misunderstood. But when rightly understood it does not oppose the other view; it confirms it. Say, if you please, that American law derives its force from the command of the sovereign. From what sovereign? From the President? Any one would scout the idea. From Congress? The very essence of constitutional limitation is that Congress cannot by its mere command make a law. From the Supreme Court? A member of that court would be the last to claim that his *ipse dixit*, or the *ipsi dixerunt* of the whole body of his colleagues, was the source of the authority of his words. From the Constitution? A constitution is not a person, but an instrument; not an authority, but an evidence of authority. The sovereign which stands behind the authority of the law is the people of the United States; the people as a collective body, in the sense in which that word was really meant by Jefferson and by Rousseau.* Not a majority of the people voting by state lines, as personified in the President; not a majority of the people voting by districts, as personified in the House of Representatives; but the people as represented by a common public sentiment which includes all good men, minorities as well as majorities, who support the government not as a selfish means for the promotion of their own interest, but as a common heritage which they accept as loyal members of a body politic, in a spirit which makes them ready to bear its burdens as well as to enjoy its benefits.

In fact, the authority of the courts, instead of going beyond the moral sense of the community,

---

* Especially by Rousseau. The purport of the *Social Contract* has been gravely misunderstood by those who have read it only at second hand. Rousseau is very careful to distinguish between that collective public sentiment which is the true will of the people, and the majority vote which is but a makeshift for trying to ascertain that will as well as we can.

and establishing obligations more severe than those which its members would impose upon themselves, as a rule keeps well within the limits set by that moral sense. It seems very doubtful whether a free community could exist unless the great majority of the members accepted moral duties much wider than the legal duties imposed upon them by judicial decisions. The obligation of a man to support his family is, to some degree, laid down by the government and enforced by it; but unless nineteen-twentieths of the community had more industrial ambition for themselves and their families than is represented by this minimum which the government prescribes, industrial progress or prosperity would be out of the question. What holds true in this field holds true in a dozen others. The vast majority of citizens find in their own personal sympathies and habits and consciences sufficient motive to compel them to perform most of their duties to society. What the courts do is to define those duties for the minority who do not understand them, and to provide an orderly means of compelling their acceptance by the yet smaller minority which repudiates them after they have been defined. When these minorities are not small, but large, the effort of the court to define and impose an obligation upon the recalcitrant community is apt to be futile. Nothing

THE BASIS OF CIVIL LIBERTY

was plainer than the decision in the Dred Scott case; yet the Fugitive Slave Law was habitually set at nought when a slave reached Northern soil. You can compel ignorant men to accept a statute; you can force bad men to obey it when they do not want to; but if a statute or a judicial decision passes the line of those duties which good and intelligent men as a body accept and impose upon themselves, it is at once nullified. The process of nullifying law has sometimes been called "passive resistance." It is in the majority of instances sufficiently described as the withdrawal of active support. In either case the result demonstrates that most of the work of government is done by men who govern themselves and say nothing about it. For if any considerable portion of these men cease to govern themselves in accordance with the law, its ineffectiveness becomes at once manifest.

When people live together in towns and cities and nations, they have to do certain things which they do not like. Bad governmental machinery may increase the number of these things, good governmental machinery may diminish them; but the necessity for doing some of them is always there. The ideal, so fondly cherished by the philosophers of a hundred years ago, of a complete system of organized non-interference, has proved impracticable. What is for the interest of the whole is often going to be against the convenience of some of the parts. There are in the last resort two means of inducing a member of the community, when thus adversely affected, to subordinate his private interest to the general good,—his own conscience, and the policeman's club. If a large majority of people are ready to be governed by their consciences, the exercise of the policeman's club becomes unnecessary, except upon that small minority who are recognized as lawbreakers. Then, and only then, can we have real democracy.

Whenever a serious political emergency arises, we find that the majority of the American people stand ready to be governed by their consciences, rather than by the more obvious dictates of self-interest. This was repeatedly proved in various stages of the anti-slavery struggle. It was proved under the perilous strain of the Electoral Commission case of 1876, when the defeated party sacrificed personal advantage and acquiesced in what seemed a violation of justice for the sake of that general stability of institutions which is essential to prevalence of right in the long run. And it is just because the American people as a body are thus prepared to accept the obligations and bear the

THE BASIS OF CIVIL LIBERTY

burdens of self-government that American democracy has been able to maintain itself.

But what would happen if a large part of our people refused to accept the principle of self-government in the true sense of the word, and undertook to assume the privileges of freedom without understanding its responsibilities?

This question came up in practice more than thirty years ago, and received an unexpected answer; an answer which confirms, in rather startling fashion, the view that, even under a democratic constitution, responsibility is a condition precedent to the exercise of freedom. At the close of our Civil War a race which had previously been held in the most abject slavery found itself suddenly emancipated. The proclamations of President Lincoln, followed by the Thirteenth Amendment of the Constitution, secured its members personal liberty. The Fourteenth Amendment almost immediately afterward gave them civil rights; and a little later the Fifteenth Amendment admitted them to full political power.

The first use which they made of their freedom was disappointing. Some abandoned their families; a much larger number abandoned their work for longer or shorter periods. Many tried to secure public offices for the performance of whose duties they were unfit. Almost all allowed their votes to be utilized by unscrupulous men as a means of establishing a corrupt and irresponsible government. The evils of this misuse of freedom became so great that after the lapse of a few years the political power of the Southern negro was abolished by a systematic nullification of the laws intended to give him the franchise; and, although many of his personal rights were allowed to remain unchallenged, he was made to feel that his freedom was a very different thing from that which he and some of his friends had anticipated. He had to begin at the bottom of the social scale and work out a capacity for freedom before he could enjoy its privileges.

As we look back on the history of the years succeeding the war, it is astonishing that men could have expected any other course of events than that which actually took place. It was not the fault of the negro; it was the fault of those who so unwisely gave him political rights without previous preparation. The history of every country of the world shows that sudden grants of liberty are followed by periods of license. This was the case in Germany at the time of the Reformation, with the advent of religious liberty; it was the case in France in the last years of the eighteenth century, with the advent

THE BASIS OF CIVIL LIBERTY 41

of political liberty; it was the case in Russia in 1863, with the advent of industrial liberty. All these instances show the impossibility of granting uncontrolled freedom to those who will not take the responsibilities that go with it. The attempt on the part of any large group of men to claim the privileges of liberty without assuming its burdens proves so destructive to the community that it has to be stopped. The North did not realize this at the close of the Civil War. The people of the North had accepted as an axiom the dictum of the Declaration of Independence that all men are created with equal rights to liberty. They of course restricted those rights in the case of minors and of insane persons. But aside from these exceptions, based, apparently at least, on physiological grounds, they recognized no limits to the principle of liberty and equality. The influx of uneducated masses into large cities had strained the application of this principle, but it had not forced men to abandon it or modify their habitual way of stating it. The population of the North, even in the cities, was so ambitious industrially that it could be persuaded to work for a living without the compulsion of a taskmaster, and so intelligent politically that the efforts of corrupt politicians to mislead the voters had generally been kept within moderate bounds. When the North saw that these conditions did not exist in the South it acquiesced in the suppression of the negro vote and in the nullification of many of the Reconstruction Acts. The North did it reluctantly; but the remarkable thing is that the North should have done it at all, at a time when war memories were so fresh and the passions and misjudgments of the war were so strong. The fact that under these circumstances the liberty of the negro was actually restricted proves more clearly than anything else could that such restriction was necessary and inevitable. How long this restriction can continue is another question. The recent industrial progress of the negro race—or at any rate of very considerable numbers of that race—puts the matter on a new basis. It looks as if we had entered an even more difficult phase of the problem than that which confronted us after the war. I shall not attempt to predict the outcome, nor to give unasked advice to those who face its difficulties most closely and understand them most clearly. But one thing should be said, and said plainly. The error of those who thirty years ago supposed that political rights could be immediately given to the negro before he had achieved industrial responsibility or moral independence was probably no greater than the error of those who to-day believe that political rights can be permanently withheld from the negro after he shall have achieved such responsibility and independence.

We have thus learned that the abstract doctrine that every one had a right to political freedom is subject in practice to certain important exceptions. We have learned that where a group of men misuse their freedom on a large scale they cannot be allowed to retain it unchallenged. But we may properly go one step farther. Instead of laying down the principle of an absolute right to freedom, and then trying to describe certain exceptional cases where this absolute right must be suspended, I believe that it will be at once more logical and more salutary if we regard the right to freedom as something proportionate to a man's capacity to use his freedom for the benefit of the community. The case of the Southern negro differs from that of many groups of white men in degree rather than in kind.* The negroes are not the only group of men who are nominally free, but really so irresponsible as to be incapable of the intelligent exercise of

* At least in its political aspect. The physiological danger of mixture of the two races is another matter. It is hard to separate these two aspects of the negro problem in our discussions or even in our thoughts; but I believe that the habitual confusion between them does a great deal of harm to our clearness of judgment, and that we ought to keep them as distinct as we can.

freedom. Whenever this combination exists it involves grave dangers, both to the individual and to the community. Freedom enables an intelligent and good man to do better things than he could do without it; and when it is thus used it stimulates progress, and intelligence, and goodness. But it must be remembered that this same freedom allows an unintelligent or bad man to do worse things than he could do without it; and that if this happens on a large scale it may prove destructive to the resources, and even to the safety, of the commonwealth. In doubtful cases, we should extend freedom rather than restrict it; for freedom, even when accompanied by some abuses, stimulates progress and makes each succeeding generation more capable of exercising it intelligently. But we cannot regard unrestrained individual liberty either as an abstract principle of political philosophy, or as an ultimate goal of human progress. It is essentially a means rather than an end; an institution rather than a principle; a help to the realization of public morality, rather than a postulate of public morality itself.

Freedom, regarded in this way, becomes a constructive force. It is not simply the absence of restraint, as is alleged by Schopenhauer and other writers who look at the subject from the standpoint

THE BASIS OF CIVIL LIBERTY

of the metaphysician rather than that of the historian. It is the substitution of self-restraint for external restraint; the substitution of a form of restraint which promotes progress for a form which represses it. Political freedom means either self-government or anarchy. In the latter case it speedily wrecks the nation that practises it. In the former case only does it last long enough to attain the dignity of a political institution. The kind of freedom which means anarchy stands condemned by its self-destructive character. The kind which means self-restraint is justified by its effect in combining order and progress.

Political thinkers are beginning to see this. We are coming to look at human history as a struggle for existence between different methods of thought and systems of morals, and to find the justification for our systems of thought and morals in the fact that they contribute to the survival and development of the race which holds them. We are coming to regard political liberty not as an abstract right, to be demanded for its own sake, as Rousseau would have demanded it; nor as a dangerous dream of unbalanced minds, to be resisted by all champions of order, as Metternich would have resisted it; but as an institution which, as different nations have worked it out for themselves, enables them to combine order with progress better than any other political system which has hitherto been devised. We have learned to judge the merits of a free government by the degree in which it realizes this combination.

But we can apply this method of analysis to other forms of freedom besides political liberty. The man who recognizes that political liberty is an institution to be judged by its results, but who at the same time regards liberty of judgment in morals as an abstract and absolute right, has apprehended but half the truth. He involves himself in contradictions at every turn. A people's politics and a people's morals are closely interdependent. The causes which justify the exercise of liberty of action in the one field are closely connected with those which justify the exercise of liberty of judgment in the other. Slavery goes hand in hand with fatalism, private property with private judgment. The attempts of Socrates and his successors to teach people the use of private judgment in morals were hampered by the fact that these people lived under a system of slavery, and had not acquired the habit of doing unpleasant labor for a remote end. The efforts of Alexander, two thousand years later, to emancipate the Russian serfs, were hampered by the fact that these serfs were fatalists, who recog-

THE BASIS OF CIVIL LIBERTY

nized no moral motive save the motive of compulsion.

The history of free institutions is a record of the gradual acceptance of the duties of self-government, moral as well as political, wherein each nation proves its right to receive freedom by accepting the responsibilities that go with it.

It is the purpose of this book to show the historical connection between liberty and responsibility in every domain of human thought. As the first and most fundamental step, we shall trace from its beginnings the theory of moral freedom; and we shall then be in a position to understand the significance of the various means used to realize this freedom, in law or in religion, in industry or in politics.

III

FREEDOM AS A RELIGIOUS CONCEPTION

THERE is among members of human society an assumption of freedom, which is apparently older, and certainly more widespread, than the chance for using that freedom under protection of the law. Its exercise may be contrary to public opinion in primitive communities; its principles may be contrary to scientific theory in advanced ones. But the individual does, as a matter of fact, assume that he has a choice of lines of action and that he exercises self-control in some shape in preferring one to another. More than this: society, from a very early period, in its theory of offences and penalties treats him as free and demands that he control himself accordingly. Even if the actual use of liberty be rendered impossible by law, and the theory which underlies it be pronounced an absurdity by science, the mere conception of freedom of the will is a social institution of the first importance. Call it a legal fiction, if you please—its importance in the history of civilization is no less real on that account.

This assumption of freedom, and the consciousness of self-restraint which goes with it, appear to be peculiar to the human race. It is very doubtful whether animals in their wild state have any corresponding feelings or habits. Of course they do a great many things involving physical inconvenience or pain which their instinct has taught them to undergo for a remote end; and they may even sacrifice their individual lives for the benefit of their families and their associates. The cat will incur unbounded danger and suffering to protect her kittens. The bee will die the most painful of deaths rather than subject the hive to pollution. But underlying all these actions there is, as far as we are able to judge, that remarkable adaptation of structure to activity which produces what we call instinct. There is a uniformity about the bee's habits of self-sacrifice, which is far different from anything that characterizes the human race. Where animals have been modified by domestication the situation is altered. We see in such cases a reflection of human lives and human habits. But with animals in their wild state, where mental processes and physical coördinations have developed side by side in the course of hundreds of generations, the two have become closely connected; and it often seems to be a physical impossibility for the individual to evade the act of self-sacrifice which has proved beneficial to the species.

With members of the human race it is far different. The physical structure does not compel the individual to conform to the code of social ethics. Among the lower animals each peculiarity of custom or habit is associated with a well marked difference of physical organism; in the human race great differences of custom subsist side by side with the very closest physical resemblance. Among the animals different systems of ethics are commonly associated with differences of species, of genus, and of order; in the human race vast varieties of difference exist within the limits of what is physiologically a single species. In some way or other man has acquired the possibility of forming groups which vary their customs without correspondingly varying their structure. His ethical development has not had to wait for a corresponding physiological development. It is this characteristic which distinguishes the evolution of mankind from the evolution of the lower animals. The main difference is not, as is so frequently said, that the human struggle for existence is a struggle between groups instead of individuals; for in more highly organized forms of animal life the subordination of the individual to the group is just as marked as in any

FREEDOM AS A RELIGIOUS CONCEPTION 51

section of the human race. The main difference is that the evolution of these human groups is a mental rather than a physical process, to be traced by the historian rather than by the neurologist, and to be explained by the study of institutions rather than by the study of tissues.

Whether there may be in the world of insect life developments more or less similar to those which are going on in human ethics, is a point which it would be difficult to settle. We have too little power of understanding the sensations of the ant or the bee to hazard a guess at the nature of their mental processes. We can see the community life of insect bodies, and can study their complex ethical system with great interest; but whether it can be accompanied, like ours, by an individual reason and individual conscience, is a matter beyond our ken. Be this as it may,—in the vertebrate world, at any rate, there is nothing which at all approximates to the mental experience of the human species.

Man's power of forming distinct ethical groups in advance of marked physiological changes has its advantages and disadvantages. It has the advantage of giving the members of the human species far greater flexibility of action, and of securing the power of rapid progress which goes with it. A group of men can in fifty years make changes of habit which an animal species—except under domestication—would hardly accomplish in five thousand. The different groups of which the race is composed can try a hundred experiments, good, bad, and indifferent, and give a chance for survival to that which proves best; while the animal species is restricted to those slow adaptations which are forced upon it by constant pressure of external circumstance. In human evolution the constructive force of imitation has been added to the destructive force of elimination which characterizes the development of the lower animals, and has proved itself much more varied and more rapid in its effects.

But all this gain is attended with some loss. The things that make the progress of the animals slow make it sure. The things which make the progress of mankind quick make it precarious. If a group of men follow a new example through sheer force of imitation, and develop a custom without waiting for changes in their structure to make it in a manner compulsory upon them, they are liable to cease to follow the new custom when it becomes disagreeable, and to lose whatever good results may have been gained from its adoption. In other words, the opportunity of progress is accompanied by the danger of reversion. To prevent such reversion social restraint becomes a necessity. If the body

FREEDOM AS A RELIGIOUS CONCEPTION

politic would preserve its ethical structure, it must prevent the individual from recklessly following out the impulses imposed by his physical structure. It is a matter of vital interest to every man to restrain himself and each of his fellows from those lapses against which his physiological constitution affords no protection—to which, indeed, it makes him perpetually liable.

The means habitually exercised to secure this restraint have been well described—or perhaps we should rather say well conjectured—by Walter Bagehot in his Physics and Politics. They are based upon the savage's belief in a complex system of magical relations, friendly or hostile, between his tribe and the various plants, animals, and ghosts, of which he has known or dreamed. All these curiously related beings, living or unliving, real or imaginary, are watchful to reward observance of the tribal traditions, and yet more watchful to punish their neglect. Under this system it becomes possible to invest with a supernatural sanction unpleasant observances which have proved beneficial to the community. The freedom from pestilence which is enjoyed by a tribe that occasionally washes is attributed to the will of some spirit related to the tribe, which insists upon this disagreeable and apparently meaningless ceremony—a spirit which will protect the members if they wash and punish them if they do not wash. For no less potent than the supernatural sanction is the collective character of the penalty. It is visited upon innocent and guilty alike. "There is no 'limited liability' in the political notions of that time; the early tribe or nation is a religious partnership, on which a rash member by a sudden impiety may bring utter ruin. If the state is conceived thus, toleration becomes wicked: a permitted deviation from the transmitted ordinances becomes simple folly,—it is a sacrifice of the happiness of the greatest number; it is allowing one individual, for a moment's pleasure or a stupid whim, to bring terrible and irretrievable calamity upon all."

In the application of this principle, the self-interest of all the other members of the tribe was enlisted to crush the offender who through selfishness or thoughtlessness was tempted to disregard the tradition. However arbitrary might be the rule, however unintentional the infraction, all violation was remorselessly punished by the whole tribe; for the whole tribe was taught to feel that the death of the offender was necessary in order to prevent the spirits from visiting upon the tribe the offence done to their authority by any single member thereof. In this stage of society the one necessary thing,

FREEDOM AS A RELIGIOUS CONCEPTION 55

more necessary than all else put together, was to build up respect for law and obedience to custom. However wasteful the process, however irrational the means used, the end justified the means and made the process necessary; for when once the savage tribe began to treat the law lightly, the result was anarchy and destruction.

But at a very early period, if not at the beginning, this external restraint upon individual conduct was supplemented by observances intended to promote the spirit of self-restraint. It is not enough for men to impose obedience to tribal custom upon others. They must be led to impose that obedience upon themselves. If they show unwillingness to do so under ordinary conditions, they must be occasionally brought back to a state where they are especially susceptible to supernatural terrors and promises. The well-fed, full-blooded, self-sufficient man is in perpetual danger of disregarding the obligations of a custom to which his physiological adaptation is imperfect; and if there are many such men in a tribe the physical penalties for violation of custom may not be sufficiently prompt to secure the implicit observance which is essential to the authority of law over the savage mind. They must be brought out of that condition of well-fed contentment. If a man is told that he should do a disagreeable thing because the spirit of his grandfather commands it, he must occasionally be brought back to the state where he sees, or thinks he sees, the spirit of his grandfather. This is the common element and purpose of the manifold forms of religious observance on the part of half-civilized peoples.* It may be accomplished by fasting, or it may be accomplished by intoxication. It may be accomplished by music and dancing, or by constrained posture and enforced vigil. The variety of means involved shows the necessity, even in this early stage of society, for something which shall counteract the daily instincts of the natural man and give force to the spiritual precepts by which the authority of custom is enforced.

But the instant we make use of self-restraint to supplement external restraint, we pave the way for the assumption of moral freedom on the part of the individual. The very observances which are used to prevent the exercise of freedom act as a recognition of its possibility. If a man is asked to restrain himself, or even put into a state where that which seemed natural and possible at one moment is made to seem unnatural and impossible at another moment, the consciousness of a choice is irresistibly

* Henry Rutgers Marshall, Instinct and Reason. New York, 1898. Chapter x, The Function of Religious Expression.

FREEDOM AS A RELIGIOUS CONCEPTION 57

brought home to him. He differs from the mere animal in having, as St. Paul says, a law in his members which is at war with the law of the spirit. The physiological adjustments inherited from remote ancestors drive him one way; the ethical rules growing up out of the recent development of his tribe drive him another way. Even though all violation of these rules be sternly repressed, the conflict of emotions still exists. It is this duality of adjustment, this separation of ethical demands and physical demands, which is the distinctive feature of human consciousness. This word consciousness has two quite distinct meanings. Sometimes it means continuous sensitiveness—a series of nervous actions which leave a permanent record in the brain of some organism. In this sense it forms no peculiarity of the human race, but is possessed in greater or less measure by a large part of the animal kingdom. But that other and narrower kind of consciousness, which implies an observation of his own mental processes on the part of the sentient individual, seems to originate in this conflict between the progressive demands of a tribal ethics and the impulses of an individual organism which has not been modified in accordance with those demands. Human consciousness grows out of the alternative or choice apparently presented by the operation of these two sets of motives; and the religious means which are used to make the ethical motive dominant emphasize the existence of this alternative and strengthen the sense of choice.

But though this subjective sense of freedom must have been present at a very early stage of society, as soon as a man separated ethical from physical motives, the objective idea of freedom as a practical possibility was still very far from being realized or admitted. Even if a man felt himself to be free, he did not tolerate such freedom on the part of others, nor did others allow its exercise on his part. Liberty was a danger to be repressed, not an agency to be utilized. From the standpoint of the tribe the mere recognition of freedom was extremely perilous. Its exercise by any one member might involve the tribe as a whole in the supernatural dangers of the wrath of the gods. The resulting evil to the tribe was about equally great whether that wrath was actually manifested or not. In the former case the tribe suffered, or thought it suffered, from the anger of the gods; in the latter case it suffered from the contempt of law which was engendered by the neglect of the gods to punish its violation. And, wholly aside from these supernatural dangers, there was a constant risk that the savage, freed from the restraint of absolute authority, would do things

FREEDOM AS A RELIGIOUS CONCEPTION

which were dangerous to discipline in times of war, and to public safety and comfort in times of peace. Both these perils had to be avoided before moral freedom could develop from a mere conception to an institution. A large part of the history of moral progress is connected with the development of means for the avoidance of these two dangers.

The chief method devised to avoid the supernatural dangers from violation of tribal morality was the system of expiation—a system which should satisfy the offended majesty of the gods without requiring the death of each offending member of the tribe. The change of conception did not allow violations of law to go unpunished, or imply that the offended gods could be satisfied with anything less than the death penalty. But it became possible to apply the death penalty vicariously—to appease the spirits by the blood, not of a member of the offending tribe, but of some one of the animals which were supposed to bear close kinship to that tribe and its members. This was the origin of the expiatory sacrifice—the sin offering of the Old Testament—as distinct from the honorific sacrifice or thank offering.

Judged by modern ideas, the whole theory of sacrificial atonement is unjust and almost sacrilegious. It is based on the assumption of divine vindictiveness. The majesty of outraged law demands a victim. If the right person can be punished, well and good; if not, the next best thing is to punish the wrong person. But to the savage mind this vicarious punishment had a real use, in allowing the life of the accidental transgressor to be saved without producing contempt for law in his mind and the mind of others. The savage had reached a mental stage where the process of atonement or expiation could be allowed; and a certain degree of mental freedom was given him thereby. For the violation of tribal custom, instead of being a thing which separated the offender forever from fellowship, was now regarded as a possible incident of life—always to be deplored, but not always to be prevented. The absolute rigidity of a religious system which tolerated no lapses on the part of any individual, gave place to the greater freedom of one which provided possibilities of atonement and forgiveness to him who had transgressed its provisions.

This development was rapidly followed by another, or rather by two others which have intermixed in varying proportions in the history of different races. One was the separation of law from morals; the other was the recognition of personal responsibility, in distinction from tribal responsibility, as the groundwork of our theory of punishment.

The separation of law from morals began as soon as sacrificial procedure was clearly defined and ordered. The attempt to provide means by which one set of crimes could be expiated led people to distinguish them from that other set of crimes which could not be expiated; to make a difference between things which offended the gods more obviously than they endangered the tribe, and things which endangered the tribe more obviously than they offended the gods. Prominent among the latter class were those offences which interfered with military discipline in time of war and with public security in time of peace. They jeopardized the community; atonement was therefore insufficient and punishment was necessary. This punishment was, however, no longer executed by the whole tribe, but by the military authorities, acting more or less directly under the advice of the priests.* The offender was punished, not because he had alienated the gods—this reason was given only in case of certain acts of sacrilege or impiety—but because

* This view holds good whether we accept the theory of Savigny, that this development of law was an orderly and spontaneous process, or the theory of Ihering, that it was accomplished by a succession of governmental acts which seemed revolutionary.

he had jeopardized the public security; not because he had involved the members of the tribe in a collective wrong, but because he had done a personal wrong to the other members of the tribe.

This idea of personal responsibility, as distinct from tribal responsibility, spread very rapidly and altered the whole character of the penological system. If offences against public security in war and in peace were personal matters, it was natural to regard many other offences in the same light, and to deal with the offender, not as a man who had involved the tribe in a quarrel with the gods, and must therefore be put to death to avert divine displeasure, but as a man who had done a greater or less degree of personal wrong, and whose penalty could be made heavy or light according to his degree of guilt. Intentional violations of tribal customs were still punished by death. They were regarded as acts of sacrilege; as sins against the Holy Ghost, which could not be forgiven. But accidental violations of law or custom, where the intent to affront the gods was absent, could be expiated by lighter penalties and forgiven by the offended deities.

The progress from polytheism to monotheism—and, in spite of many reversions and lapses, the history of civilization is marked by such progress—inclined people more and more toward this rational classification of offences and penalties. If there were many gods, at war with one another, each god was necessarily anxious to vindicate his authority against the least appearance of neglect or contempt. Where there was but one god, his authority was too strong to be jeopardized by accidental pieces of neglect, and the penalties of such a religion could be reserved for those who habitually or intentionally violated the more serious articles of the moral code.

And thus out of the old chaos of tribal customs, which were neither law in the modern sense nor morals in the modern sense, there was developed a systematic set of penalties for specific offences. Where these offences endangered military discipline they were defined by military authorities. Where they endangered public safety in time of peace, the military and the religious authorities shared in defining them—the former influence being generally stronger among the nations of the Western world, and the latter among those of the Eastern world. Where they affected the foundations of morality rather than the immediate needs of discipline or public security, the definition was almost completely in the hands of the priests. But in all these cases there was a tendency to use the organized military force of the community for the punishment and represssion of these offences. In place of the old-fashioned lynch law, administered by the whole tribe under the influence of blinding passion, there was an orderly proof of guilt and an orderly application of the corresponding penalty.

This system of penalties for offences against public security, of procedure for proving them, of definitions of wrong for which the various penalties would be visited, and of definitions of right corresponding to these definitions of wrong, received the name of law. The residuum which was left of the old body of tribal customs, for whose violation no specific penalty could be provided other than disapproval or ostracism on the part of the tribe and personal displeasure on the part of the gods, received the name of morals.

Morality, after law has thus been separated from it, differs from the older body of tribal morality in several ways. It has less visible force behind it. It allows the individual greater chance to break its rules. But it can at the same time extend those rules over a far wider sphere of human activity than would be possible if it relied primarily on physical force and took cognizance only of those offences where the slightest deviation from its code could be summarily punished. There is a story of an Eton head master, in the old days when flogging was

FREEDOM AS A RELIGIOUS CONCEPTION 65

constant and universal, who expounded Scripture as follows: " 'Blessed are the pure in heart.' Mind that, boys. The Bible says it is your duty to be pure in heart. If you are not pure in heart, I'll flog you." This exposition represents perfectly the mental attitude of the savage world, which saw no sense in a precept that went beyond the domain of outward acts to be required and of physical penalties for non-compliance. But a large part of the morality of civilized nations deals with spheres of conduct where it is not always possible to prevent deviations from the standard, to prove the existence of offences, or to visit adequate physical penalties. The fact that modern society has law as well as morals—that it has means of preventing or repressing acts which furnish a direct menace to public security—allows it to tolerate a number of acts which it disapproves but which do not menace public security. It can without overwhelming danger to itself sit still and wait for the slow working out of the more subtle moral penalties which are to visit the offender.

What is this moral penalty for violations of public sentiment of which the law cannot take cognizance?

In early times people thought that it was the displeasure of the gods, as manifested by retribution in this life. In this theory there was the great difficulty that the good man did not always enjoy external prosperity. The whole book of Job is an interesting illustration of the difficulties which this fact presented when people begun to reason about it. And yet it is significant that after all the really able reasoning in the book of Job, the author finally finds it necessary to make good the loss of Job's children, and give him twice as many cattle as he possessed before the days of his adversity,—showing a certain want of confidence in his moral conclusions unless they are emphasized by a tangible token of return to favor. In a later stage of thought, some men have looked to a future life as a place where matters should be set right—where the bad who had enjoyed worldly prosperity should be punished, and the good who had suffered adversity should be rewarded; and others, who have not found their minds able to accept the evidence of such a system of future rewards and punishments, have thought that the good man might seek his reward in the approval of good men, even where they were relatively few; and in the approval of his own conscience, where there was none but himself good.

But whatever the sanction and whatever the means of enforcement of moral law, there is in all

FREEDOM AS A RELIGIOUS CONCEPTION 67

these modern systems an acceptance of—nay, an insistence upon—moral responsibility. You are punished for your offences not, as was the case under the old system, because an outraged god wishes to take vengeance upon the tribe, and you are sacrificed to his rage; but because you, as an individual, have the choice between doing right and doing wrong, and have done wrong. You are allowed to take the choice, because a wider and higher morality can be worked out in this way than in any other. The conflict between selfish and unselfish motives in the human heart is frankly recognized, and is used as an instrument for bringing ethical obligation home to the individual. We no longer live under a moral despotism which says: "You must do this; you must do that." Precepts which take this shape are not morality, they are law; and, as we shall see in a subsequent lecture, only a portion of the law at that. Within the domain of morality a man is told: "You may do this, or you may do that. You may choose the selfish side, you may choose the unselfish side. Yours is the responsibility of deciding, yours the guilt if you decide in the way which religion or morality disapproves." This is the process of education used by parents on a small scale as soon as their children are old enough to take responsibility. It is used by the community on a larger scale in judging the action of its members in public and private business, as long as they have the strength and intelligence to exercise independence of judgment. To a few who are notably deficient in ordinary brain power the community gives the name of insane persons. It releases them from responsibility, and in case of need subjects them to physical restraint as a means of preventing harm to themselves and others. The rest of the world it treats as morally free and holds morally responsible.

In so doing it accomplishes two ends. In the first place, it secures more intelligent conduct than is possible when every one is held in leading strings. In some cases the moral authority of the community loses by the process, in others it gains; but on the whole the gain is much greater than the loss. Relieve a boy or man from tutelage, and you make it possible for him to become much worse than he otherwise might; but if he will control himself by force of his own will, without waiting for yours to dominate him, you not only save wasteful effort on your own part, but you can rely on him to carry his goodness into a number of fields where your supervision would be inadequate and fruitless. In matters of law, the man who always has a policeman to watch him may be relied upon to be good in the policeman's presence. You cannot tell what would happen when the policeman goes to sleep, or when the man can run faster than the policeman. The analogy holds perfectly in the matter of morality, and is one of the reasons why theories of personal responsibility and freedom of the will are not only tolerated, but actually taught.

There is, however, another reason, and perhaps an equally powerful one, for insistence upon these theories. As has been already said, the principle of equity, of justice, of payment for personal merit or demerit, is prominent in our whole judicial system. But you cannot, without violation of this theory of justice, punish a man for a thing for which he is not responsible. If the malefactor was compelled by a higher power to commit wrongs, it is not for this higher power to condemn him. If the sinner sins, not by his own choice but under the influence of irresistible motives, the ruler that punishes him in this world, and the god that punishes him in the next, are both guilty of violations of justice. We may try to explain our penological system as a method for the prevention of crime, our theological system as an explanation of the order of a universe, and disclaim in either case any obligation to be just to individuals. But the moral sense of those who reason about these things today demands some distributive fairness in the allotment of rewards and punishments. If a man really has a choice this necessity is met. To save its sense of justice, while imposing physical penalties and preaching moral ones, society asserts the existence of such a choice and of the responsibility that goes with it. These facts go far to explain the general teaching and general acceptance of the theory of freedom of the will. From the standpoint of modern science this theory is little short of an absurdity. From the standpoint of modern morals, it is little short of a necessity. The community must compel its members to exercise self-control, and must justify itself for punishing them when they fail to exercise it. Both of these results are secured by the teaching of the freedom of the will.

This theory, which regards the freedom of the will as an institution rather than as a metaphysical conception, finds much to justify it in history. While it is very difficult to enter into the thoughts and feelings of peoples in a state of civilization less advanced than our own, it seems quite clear that the teaching and acceptance of free will has gone hand in hand with the development of self-control and sense of justice. This historical explanation of the idea of free will seems more satisfactory than the psychological explanation

FREEDOM AS A RELIGIOUS CONCEPTION

current among a group of writers of whom Leslie Stephen may serve as an example. These writers regard the freedom of the will as an inference which we draw from our own mental uncertainty. We do not know, for instance, whether it will be our right hand or our left hand which we next lift; and from our own ignorance on this point we assume that it is altogether and wholly undetermined. Now it may very well be that this sort of uncertainty has its effect in securing more ready and universal acceptance of the theory than would otherwise have been possible. It is quite conceivable that a few men, reasoning on a basis of this uncertainty, might have worked out for themselves a metaphysical theory of free will on that basis alone. But its universal acceptance as a working hypothesis in daily life, even on the part of those who do not assent to it as a scientific principle, is due primarily to its overwhelming importance in the history of morals. By the imposition of that sense of responsibility which goes with the assumption of freedom, society is able to extend its moral restraints over those spheres of action which can only be regulated by self-control; and is able also to impose the necessary penalties, spiritual or temporal, upon wrong-doers of various classes, without violating its own sense of justice. The theory of freedom of the will is a legal conception devised and adapted for this purpose. It is not an inference which a man draws from his own uncertainty as to what he is going to do. It is a thing which has been taught him by the community, and which he in turn teaches to other members of the community as a means of securing responsibility and rational conduct over a wider range of fields than has been possible under any other intellectual system. Judged in this way, the freedom of the will is not a postulate of all thinking, as its advocates would have us believe, nor an absurdity destructive of all scientific thinking, as would be charged by its opponents; but a legal conception, developed in the history of the human race as a means of securing that moral responsibility which is necessary for the exercise of all forms of legal and industrial freedom in the complex life of civilized communities.

IV

FREEDOM AS A LEGAL INSTITUTION

A HUNDRED years ago a great deal was said about the gradual passage of the human race from a system of authority to a system of liberty. It was supposed that in early ages different tribes and peoples had been subjected to compulsion which prevented them from doing what they wanted to do and had a natural right to do; but that in later times they gradually came to the enjoyment of that right and gained the power to act as they pleased. As long as democracy was not tried on a large scale, this theory of the nature of political progress did little harm. But whenever it was extensively put in practice—whenever, in short, nations undertook to exercise freedom without self-imposed responsibility—it made trouble. As long as the so-called democracies of Greece were really aristocracies, managed by conservative men who lived in the fear of the gods, matters went fairly well, although—or perhaps because—the amount of liberty actually enjoyed in such communities was not very great.

But when the influences of luxury and the teachings of sophistical philosophers led the Athenian youth to make their own inclinations the real guide of their conduct as well as the nominal one, the Athenian state went to pieces. Similar consequences have followed the irresponsible exercise of liberty in all other places, whether it worked in the direction of self-indulgence, as at Rome, or of religious fanaticism, as at Münster, or of political violence, as at Paris. The result was in each case suicidal.

A better statement of the history of modern freedom, and one which would command more universal assent among critical observers at the beginning of the twentieth century, is that it represents a passage from a system of obligations imposed by the community to a system of self-imposed obligations. Duty, in the early stages of society, is enforced by lynch law. In the later stages of society it is enforced by the individual conscience. It is not that the obligations recognized are narrower or less exacting in the latter case than in the former. They tend in fact to become wider and more exacting. But the method of enforcement allows the individual to get at things in his own way with less interference from others. We have passed from a system of status, where each man was born into a

FREEDOM AS A LEGAL INSTITUTION 75

set of legal rights and duties imposed upon him for all time, to a system of contract, where each man's rights and duties are largely those which he has made for himself. This change has not enabled a man to relieve himself from obligations to his fellow men. It has allowed those obligations to take forms suited to the varied powers of the individual and the varied needs of society.

In one sense, this system of self-imposed obligations is a mere corollary of the theory of moral freedom as developed in the last lecture. But it is a corollary or inference which it is not always easy for people to draw. It is one thing to accept the theory that each man is responsible for his own conduct. It is a very different thing to sit calmly by and see him indulge in conduct at variance with our preconceived notions. In other words, the recognition of freedom of the will does not carry with it either civil liberty or religious toleration. It is often treated as an abstract principle, useful in preaching to others the duty of self-control, or in justifying us for punishing them when they do not control themselves in the manner which society approves, but not compelling us to grant them any actual freedom of deed, of speech, or even of thought.

Indeed, the notion of basing real liberty of

thought or action upon personal responsibility is a comparatively modern one. In the early stages of society most of the liberty which existed was based upon irresponsibility. If a man enjoyed freedom of action, it was because he was too strong to be subjected to the laws. Deeds of violence, for which the weak man would have been put to death, in the case of the strong man went unpunished or were condoned for a wholly inadequate fine. And if a man was allowed any freedom of thought—or any freedom in the expression of his thoughts—it was for a somewhat similar reason. It was because the contagious influence of his frenzy compelled the priesthood to tolerate his utterances, whether they would or no.

What were the steps by which society passed from this early condition, where all freedom, legal and moral, lay outside of the domain of normal law, to one like the present, where freedom of action is greatest for him who can furnish the most security for abiding by the law, and where freedom of thought is largest to him who is most rational in its expression?

It is not easy to answer such large questions as these within the limits of a single lecture. But we can at least trace some of the stages in this double process of evolution.

FREEDOM AS A LEGAL INSTITUTION 77

It is a characteristic of all early communities that each man was born into a certain set of rights and duties from which he could never free himself. This system of status, or caste, is a survival of the old tribal organization when law and morals were undistinguished; when social arrangements existed by the authority of the gods; and when any attempt to disturb them was an act of impiety or sacrilege. When law was first separated from morals, many of the arrangements and the penalties remained for the moment unchanged.

But it was not long before an alteration in the character of the legal penalties began to take place. Where one man had wronged another unintentionally, it became possible not only to inflict punishment, but to exact compensation. Instead of the fine which was exacted for an offence against public order, the community could compel the payment of damages to make good the loss to the person injured. Even where the wrong was intentional, the idea of compensation could enter into the penalty or supplement it. When once the legal authorities grasped this possibility of using a civil remedy instead of a criminal one, it became possible to allow to any man who could pay substantial damages a degree of personal liberty which was not possible under a system where every infraction of others' rights, even when accidental, must be treated as a crime and visited with criminal penalties to prevent its recurrence.

From the development of civil damages it was but a short step to the system of contracts. The essential idea of a contract is that one or both of the parties thereto agrees to perform a certain service at a future time. The obligation which a man assumes in a contract is voluntary until he has made the agreement. After he has made the agreement society will compel him to pay damages for its breach, just as it would compel him to pay damages for the breach of any of the other rights of his fellow citizens. It is therefore, in its very essence, a combination of freedom and responsibility. It is a means which the community can adopt for getting work done by the voluntary assumption of obligations on the part of its members. These obligations they can be compelled to perform, or at the very worst they can be compelled to furnish compensation to the other party for their non-performance. Among the many brilliant contributions of the Roman lawyers to the progress of civilization, there was probably none so wide-reaching as their development of the theory of contracts. For wherever this theory was applied it taught people that the exercise of freedom involved the assumption of responsibility, and could be safely combined with it.

This lesson was not easy to learn, and the Roman lawyers did not succeed in teaching it to the civilized world for all time. The irruption of the barbarians into Europe brought with it, under the feudal system, a nearly complete return to the old theory of status or congenital obligation. But with the close of the feudal period the ideas of the Roman law were taken up and widely expanded. The power of making a contract under the old Roman empire had been practically, though not theoretically, limited to a few men; to those men, namely, who could furnish security for the performance of their part of the obligation. A could not give B a present consideration for the sake of B's future promise, unless he was sure that B could either perform his promise or could compensate A for the failure. The mere criminal remedy of putting B in prison would not protect A, nor offer him sufficient inducement for furnishing B with that consideration which was the basis of the contract. Under the economic conditions which prevailed in the Roman world, the power of making contracts belonged chiefly to freemen, and indeed to that minority of the freemen who enjoyed the benefits of slavery,— the planters of Rome, as distinct from the poor whites. At the close of the Middle Ages, however, the reintroduction of the idea of contractual obligation as a basis for social order was accompanied by a system of emancipation—complete in some countries, partial in others—which gave the laborer a certain amount of property right in the product of his toil. This substitution of industrial for military tenure put a much larger number of people in a position to furnish security for the performance of contracts. It enabled the people as a whole, instead of a privileged few, to enjoy the system of education in responsibility which marks the growth of contract law.

For our modern law of contract is a most valuable system of moral education, operating alike upon lawyers and upon laymen, and enabling us to make progress both in our judicial ethics and in our general tone of public morality. The whole English commercial law of the seventeenth and eighteenth centuries, with its distinctions, sometimes fine drawn but always well drawn, in matters like agency or warranty, competence or negligence, involves a systematic enforcement of responsibility under the forms of freedom. If we wish to see what this legal development has accomplished in the way of introducing responsibility, we have only to contrast our standards of practice and ethics in those lines where commercial law has been developing for centuries with those where its application is comparatively new. If I sell a cow on the basis of certain representations, and these representations prove to be false, the law holds me to an implied contract of warranty, even if I have explicitly disclaimed any intention to warrant the animal. If I sell a railroad under similar circumstances the law offers the sufferer no corresponding remedy; and no small section of the public applauds the seller for the shrewdness which he has displayed in the transaction. If I use an individual position of trust to enrich myself at the expense of others, the law will compel me to make restitution, even where criminal intent was absent. But if I profit by similar errors in the management of a corporate trust, the difficulty of bringing the responsibility home is very great indeed.

These facts and the evils connected with them are notorious. Any improvement in these matters which shall bring the conduct of associations—whether public or private, of capitalists or of laborers—up to the same moral level which characterizes the conduct of individuals, involves a combined legal and moral process. The same conception of the duty of agents and trustees which now prevails in the dealings of individuals with one another, and constitutes part of our standards of morality and gentlemanly honor, must be adopted by the courts and accepted by the people in dealing with the affairs of corporations. There has already been a decided movement in that direction. The standards of corporation law and morals were better in 1880 than they were in 1860. They were better in 1900 than they were in 1880. Much, however, remains to be accomplished before they reach a satisfactory stage. Until this process is complete we shall witness alternations between reckless license of corporate management on the one hand and socialistic agitation for control on the other. The problem will not be solved until, by the gradual acceptance of responsibility, we have achieved that combination of liberty and self-control which is the basis of freedom as a legal institution. When corporate agents assume the same kind of moral duties and responsibilities that are now assumed by private individuals, then—and not till then—may we expect that they will have the same immunity from legislative interference.

It is the ideal of a free community to give liberty wherever people are sufficiently advanced to use it in ways which shall benefit the public, instead of in ways which will promote their own pleasure at the public expense. And it has been the practice of the most successful communities to go farther than this, and give freedom somewhat in advance of this ethical development, wherever, by suits for damages or enforcement of contractual obligations, the losses arising from misuse of freedom could be so far brought home to the individual offender as to prevent him from repeating his error at public expense. Liberty is directly advantageous wherever the ethical development of the community fits people for its use; it is likely to prove indirectly advantageous wherever there is a fair promise that they can be taught to improve their ethical standards in the immediate future.

This statement of the limits of civil liberty differs somewhat, in theory at least, from that of John Stuart Mill. Mill makes a fundamental distinction between self-regarding actions, which affect almost exclusively the individual immediately concerned, and actions which are not primarily or chiefly self-regarding, so that they affect the community more than they do the individual. In the former case, he says, we can allow the very widest degree of liberty; in the latter case we must have a much larger degree of restriction. With all deference to the eminent writers by whom this theory has been upheld, I cannot think that it is possible thus to set apart any group of actions as self-regarding.

84 FREEDOM AND RESPONSIBILITY

Every kind of act may affect others overwhelmingly. The utterance of a thought would be considered a self-regarding action; the picking of a pocket an action which affected others. Yet it will not infrequently happen that one man by expressing his real thoughts to another may do him and do the community a more irreparable harm than if he had picked the other man's pocket. The question of the degree of liberty which can be allowed in any given field turns more upon the character of the actors than upon the character of the acts. The system of legal arrangements for the promotion of liberty attempts not so much to divide men's actions into different classes, in one of which liberty can be allowed and in the other of which it cannot be allowed, as to take account of men's characteristics in such a way as to leave the people free or to educate them for freedom in those fields where such freedom or education is possible.

The difficulty of applying Mill's classification is seen when we look at the history of freedom of thought. If there is one form of activity which more than all others Mill and his school would treat as self-regarding, it is the activity of a man's brain. Yet freedom of thought has been of slower growth than freedom of action; and even to the present

FREEDOM AS A LEGAL INSTITUTION

day it presents harder problems for the theorist to deal with.

In the earliest stages of social development, free thought was obviously not a self-regarding action. It was not tolerated, and it could not be; because it was the very thing which most offended the gods, and thus brought destruction upon every member of the tribe. It was worse than illegal conduct. For conduct which violated the code of tribal custom might be a mere accident—in which case the gods would perhaps be satisfied with some expiation short of the death of the offender. But a thought which was at variance with the theory on which these tribal customs were supported was not accidental. It was a bold and deliberate defiance of the authority of the gods—an act of sacrilege of the worst form. The effect of this view is manifested in the terrible frenzy and cruelty which, down to comparatively modern times, has characterized religious persecution.

But the very observances which were adopted as a means for securing the authority of the priests over the tribe paved the way for occasional defiance of this authority. The fastings and ceremonies which strengthened the influence of the priesthood provided also a receptive audience for persons, within that priesthood or outside of it, who might believe themselves possessed of new revelations to communicate. If a man was placed in the condition where he would see the spirit of his grandfather, he was likely to see some other things not dreamed nor intended by those who brought him to this state. A time of frenzy gave every opportunity for an innovator to say things which at soberer times people would not have dared to listen to, and which he himself might not have dared to think.* A man of oratorical temperament, who at other seasons would have been stoned to death as a blasphemer, might now be welcomed as a prophet. This was the beginning of liberty of teaching. Where the priests represented scientific conservatism, the prophets represented scientific progress. It is needless to say that there was none too much love between priests and prophets. The former would as a rule willingly have exterminated the latter. But over and over again it is related that "they feared the people." The new word which the prophet had uttered had received such a hearing that there was greater

* This was the one thing which gave progressive men and progressive views a fair chance. It was probably on this principle that the ancient Macedonians based their custom, which so impressed Herodotus, of never taking any important action till they had discussed it twice—once when they were sober and once when they were drunk.

FREEDOM AS A LEGAL INSTITUTION 87

danger to the priestly authority in its suppression than in the unwilling toleration of its continuance.

But how should this toleration be justified without weakening the whole authority of the law? The case could not be met by a system of sacrificial expiation. In the first place, if the progressive thought of the prophets was an offence, no expiation would have been sufficient to atone for it; and even if it had been sufficient, the prophets would have been the last ones to coöperate in making such atonement. The very essence of their claim, which gave them their hold over the people, was that they were possessed of a divine revelation which it was a merit and not a sin to preach. Under these circumstances the priests adopted the simple method of treating the prophet as legally irresponsible. They said, in short, that he was crazy; and this explanation was quite readily accepted. Even at the present day, the majority of hard-headed business men believe that poets, professors, and other classes of idealists have a bee in their bonnets; and if this is true now, when men of these classes are held amenable to the law of the land, much more necessarily was it the case when they were openly proclaimed as madmen and encouraged, if not compelled, to adapt their conduct to the character thus thrust upon them.

It may be remarked in passing that this ancient conception of insanity was not so totally different from the modern one, regarded from the legal side. We have a theory that the question of insanity in murder trials is proved by medical examination. But in a very large number of cases the diagnosis is based on the circumstances of the murder itself. We use the term insanity as a convenient excuse for men whose acts and feelings are so remote from the usual run of human experience as to lead the jury to think that the authority of the law will be better upheld by excusing them than by hanging them. The difference between ancient and modern conceptions lies rather in the degree of liberty which we propose to allow the insane man afterward. The ancient priesthood held that if a man was insane and could not be punished he was therefore free; the modern court holds that if a man is insane and cannot be punished his freedom must be restricted on that account, in order to prevent a recurrence of the dangerous act.

Free thought based on the claim of insanity was better than no free thought at all. But it gave an unfortunate sort of monopoly of the privileges of liberty to those who were least competent to use them wisely. If a leader arrived who was obviously not insane, but clear-headed and of sound judgment, who did not take the guise of a madman but accepted the obligations and duties of daily life, the religious system provided no place for him. The very qualities which distinguished Jesus of Nazareth above the prophets who had preceded him as a religious reformer stood in the way of his acceptance among the Jewish authorities of his generation. People began by reviling him; they ended by crucifying him. "John came neither eating nor drinking, and ye say, He hath a devil. The Son of Man came eating and drinking, and ye say, Behold a glutton and a winebibber, a friend of publicans and sinners." Over and over again among the peoples of the East the dangers which arose from having leaders of thought more or less insane, or at any rate compelling them to pretend to be more or less insane, have manifested themselves, and still manifest themselves down to the present day. The system causes the Oriental armies to be commanded by fanatics, capable at times of rousing their followers to violent acts, but incapable of sustained judgment in directing the employment of means toward a practical end. It causes Oriental society to be burdened with vast numbers of half insane and wholly irresponsible mendicants—religious zealots, who have something of the external characteristics of prophets, but very little of their internal character. The system prevents moral stagnation, but at the more or less habitual sacrifice of public order, public economy, and public security.

When our religious thinkers had advanced far enough for us to regard sin as a personal offence, which brought down the wrath of God upon the individual, rather than as a collective offence, which caused God to punish the whole tribe without discrimination, the way was open for tolerating free thought among men who were not insane. Even those who regarded progressive ideas as acts of immorality on the part of the thinker did not find themselves compelled to kill him in order to prevent the penalty of his impiety from being visited upon themselves. The progressive thinker could be treated as one who did not jeopardize the safety of all his associates by his irreligious utterances. Perhaps it might prove that his teaching was not so wholly wrong after all. The authorities might safely say concerning the innovators, as Gamaliel said in the trial of the Apostles: "Refrain from these men and let them alone: for if this counsel or this work be of men it will come to nought; but if it be of God ye cannot overthrow it: lest haply ye be found even to fight against God." Where the separation of legal and moral authority had become at all complete—where, in other words, a change of

FREEDOM AS A LEGAL INSTITUTION 91

mythology did not weaken public security—this was the logical and natural ground to take.

But even when we have accepted this theoretical view of the case, we may fall far short of the actual toleration of free thought. We may admit that the impiety of an individual does not in itself constitute a danger to public security, and that the holding of a wrong opinion constitutes in itself no menace to social order, and nevertheless be extremely intolerant of these opinions in practice—either because we think that the holding of opinions which we consider wrong will harm the individual himself, or because we think that the inevitable expression of those opinions will harm the community.

In early stages of society, or with undeveloped systems of legal procedure, the first of these ideas is the dominant one. Where law is imperfectly separated from morals, and where the powers of church and state are closely intermingled, it is inevitable that this should be the case. If a man puts himself in danger of eternal punishment by a certain line of thought, it is not an evidence of breadth of mind, but an evidence of scandalous indifference to his fate, to leave him to pursue that line of thought undisturbed. Galileo was forbidden to teach that the earth revolved around the sun because it was believed to be wrong for him to think that the earth revolved around the sun. Socrates was condemned to lose his life, not so much because he kept a school in which the youth were systematically instructed—though this played a part in the proceedings—but because the dæmonism which he was supposed to teach savored of impiety to those who had been brought up with conservative religious ideas. There are always misguided friends of the free thinker who are so concerned about his future welfare that they cannot let him subject himself to the penalties of his impiety without doing their utmost to interfere—friends who will impose legal restraints upon him if they can, and failing this, will use to the utmost extent the less tangible but no less effective restraints of personal entreaty or of public disapproval. Those of us who claim to be most enlightened in this matter of toleration of opinion cannot rid ourselves of the habits of intolerance inherited from our ancestors. If we are inclined for a moment to doubt this last proposition, we have only to consider how much of our own time has been spent in indignation against other people for holding views which were different from our own, even in cases where there was no particular chance that the views of either of us would have any influence on the external acts of the other. Neither philosophers nor scientists are exempt from

FREEDOM AS A LEGAL INSTITUTION 93

this difficulty. The *odium theologicum* extends to every school of thought. Professor W. K. Clifford argues that the right of private judgment is an absolute one, with an almost vituperative scorn of those who exercise private judgment to the extent of differing with him in this opinion. The difficulty of learning to mind our own business in the matter of interference with other people's thoughts is so great, even where we find actual tolerance of differences of religious or scientific opinion, that we are only too apt to discover that this is the result of apathy rather than of intelligence.

But as the conception of law has become more and more clearly defined, and the line between church and state more distinct, there has been an increasing reluctance on the part of the government to lend its aid in suppressing opinions which, however dangerous they may be to the souls of those who hold them, do not constitute an immediate menace to public security and social order. And slowly but surely this increasing conservatism in the use of legal penalties leads to a corresponding conservatism in the administration of theological penalties. Where the law will hang a man for every affront to civil authority, real or supposed, the theologians have no difficulty in persuading people that the gods will punish all transgressors in an equally bloodthirsty spirit. There is in every tribe and every nation an almost necessary correspondence between its moral system and its legal system. The character of its chiefs will be reflected in the character of its gods, and vice versa. If the system of legal penalties is vindictive and arbitrary, the system of spiritual penalties will be vindictive and arbitrary also. If the system of legal penalties is rational, judging the offender by his intent and giving him fair opportunity to argue his case, this habit will be reflected in the theological arguments and the conception of the divine penalty. In the Jokes of the Lacedæmonians, Plutarch—if it really be Plutarch who made this curious collection of ancient wit—tells how a Lacedæmonian remarked, as they passed the contribution box, "I have no use for gods that are poorer than I am." No nation can accept a morality on the part of its spiritual rulers inferior to that which characterizes its earthly ones. Rational law carried with it the development of rational theology. It relieved us from the fear that the good man would be eternally punished for a mistake of doctrine. It made the eradication of those mistakes no longer a duty which a man owed to his friends, but a matter of private judgment, to be decided on questions of expediency. It deprived our habits of intolerance of the justifica-

FREEDOM AS A LEGAL INSTITUTION 95

tion which they had when they were part of a legal and theological system, and left them standing isolated in the modern world as an anomalous survival of ancient prejudices.

But even under the most advanced legal systems and the most logical methods of thought, it is impossible to make toleration of differences of opinion as absolute a right as some people assume. For freedom to hold an opinion is meaningless unless it carries with it freedom to express the opinion. Nations with advanced legal systems very rarely interfere with opinion in its former aspect. In the latter aspect they frequently have occasion to restrict or suppress it. The Roman law persecuted the Christians, not so much for their religious opinions as for their habit of holding irresponsible public assemblies. This was a thing of which the Roman authorities were always jealous; and they were especially jealous of these assemblies of the Christians because the theories of divine sovereignty therein set forth often seemed to menace the legal right of the emperor. The persecution, or alleged persecution, of scientific men in some of our modern communities is not, in general, an attempt to prevent them from holding such opinions as they please concerning the evolution of species, or the proper material for a dollar, or the physiological effects of alcohol, but to prevent them from making use of official position to teach these opinions, and drawing a salary for so doing.

All these instances show how hard it is to separate the question of the right of free thought from the question of illegal activity, or even to be quite sure which of these things is being infringed and restricted. If a man is deprived of a teaching position because he advocates the Darwinian theory or the silver standard, his friends will regard it as an attack upon liberty of thought; his enemies will consider it a protection of public morality. The trustees who remove such an officer will probably make the mistake of under-estimating the possibility of good which results from freedom, but they will be right in considering the act of teaching as being not a self-regarding one but one whose good or bad use involves good or evil to others besides the teacher, and as regarding themselves as having special duties of interference if evil is done in the exercise of this function. The remedy for this state of things is not to be found by trying to draw more clearly the line between actions which concern the teacher himself and actions which concern others. This is an impossibility. Things which might be harmless if uttered by a teacher of one subject to pupils of advanced age might be utterly demoralizing if set forth by a teacher of another subject to pupils of another stage of training. Nor can we attempt to mitigate the evil by changing the character of the board of trustees. The particular form of the board of control makes a difference with the direction in which the restraint is exercised, rather than with the amount of such restraint. The trustees of an ecclesiastical college concern themselves chiefly with religious opinions, those of a state college with political opinions, those of a private foundation with economic opinions; but the actual degree of liberty allowed depends upon the stage of intellectual development which has been reached by the teacher and by the community about him. The amount of freedom which can be tolerated depends upon the responsibility of the speaker, and perhaps to a yet greater degree upon the responsibility of the community in making use of the doctrines which he preaches.

There was a time when a considerable part of the anarchists of America advocated doctrines of forcible resistance to authority which were not consonant with the American Constitution. For many years they were allowed to do this without molestation. It was supposed that the utterance of these sentiments did little harm—that they were mere talk, and nothing more. But when the people who heard these speeches began to murder officials, the case was different. The public expression of certain views was summarily stopped by treating the men who expressed them as guilty of the crime of incitement to murder. It was in vain for these men to plead, as they perhaps could conscientiously do, that they were simply uttering theories about the government, and that a man had a right to utter any theory he pleased. This sentiment would hold good as long as the audience was sufficiently rational not to try to put the theories in practice. When this condition ceased to exist, the possibility of freedom was diminished.

This case of the anarchists is important as illustrating quite clearly the conditions which limit the exercise of toleration. Speaking broadly, there is no question that toleration is a good thing. The argument of Carlyle, that nine men out of ten will judge badly, and that they should therefore follow a leader who can judge well, instead of pursuing independent courses of their own, proves less than it appears to; for the mistakes that the nine men make serve as a warning to prevent others from following their example, while the good judgment of the tenth man is a permanent contribution to progress. As Morley well says, the system of toleration lays down the main condition of finding

FREEDOM AS A LEGAL INSTITUTION 99

your hero; to leave all ways open to him, because no man knows by which way he should come. But there is this important truth to be emphasized on the other side: that the amount of private judgment which the members of a nation can advantageously or even safely exercise depends upon their own moral character. That degree of freedom which in one stage of society, or among men of one kind, serves as a means to progress, would in another stage and with other men loosen all foundations of social cohesion and constitute a relapse into anarchy.

To a certain extent, every one recognizes this truth. Every one sees that discussion with young children or with immature races must be handled in a different fashion from that which would be permissible with men of more advanced age or civilization. It is the central idea of Bagehot's Physics and Politics that institutions and habits of thought had to be so arranged as to produce cohesion before there was any room for liberty. What Bagehot perhaps inadequately realizes, and what many other political writers far more conspicuously fail to realize, is that this need of maintaining social cohesion is a perpetual one. It is not a thing which has been established once for all in the course of prehistoric or early historic ages, and may now be left to take care of itself. We have not by the labors of our ancestors attained a degree of discipline which makes society permanently safe from disorganization. Athens was a well established and highly organized state; yet the teachings of Socrates at Athens were followed by a Macedonian conquest. The Italian republics had well developed traditions and were under the authority of a powerful church; but the revival of learning in Italy was followed, at no very long interval, by a decadence in all that had made Italy great. The nineteenth century has witnessed a third experiment in introducing similar theories of self-interest and private judgment. This experiment is made under more favorable conditions than its predecessors, because the greater distribution of property, the wider understanding of contractual obligations, and the habits taught by the Protestant churches of exercising private judgment on matters outside the domain of selfish interest have increased our power of using the freest thought without interfering with that discipline which is necessary to the work of civilized society. But with all these advantages, it is going to be a very critical experiment to teach the people as a body that they are free to think what they like and to do what they like. Just as the possibility of industrial freedom depends upon a man's readiness to assume the obligations of contract and his responsibility in standing up to them, even when they work to his own inconvenience, so the possibility of intellectual liberty is dependent upon a man's readiness to accept the responsibilities involved in the use of private judgment. He must be prepared to exercise that judgment on a Stoic rather than an Epicurean basis; making the good of society the standard of his moral conduct even when this standard shall work to his own inconvenience or hurt.

V

FREEDOM AS A FOUNDATION OF ETHICS

THE liberals, or champions of liberty, include two somewhat distinct groups: the advocates of toleration and the advocates of individualism. The former group believes in allowing people a large measure of liberty in managing their own affairs, because it thinks that their errors as well as their successes will teach the community a lesson for the future, and thus contribute indirectly to its progress. The latter group believes in allowing people a still larger measure of liberty, even in affairs which are not distinctly their own, because it thinks that the enlightened selfishness of individuals contributes directly to the good of the body politic. The former would allow people to be free to make their own mistakes, in the belief that temporary error is self-corrective; the latter would encourage people to pursue their own interests, in the belief that enlightened selfishness promotes the common interest. The former group, which makes freedom a means of progress, is represented by men

FREEDOM AS A FOUNDATION OF ETHICS

like Mill and Morley; the latter, which makes it a basis of ethics, is represented by men like Bastiat and Clifford.

Of course these two groups are not wholly separate. There are a great many men who believe both in toleration and in self-interest, and can with fairness base their advocacy of liberty on either ground which may prove more convenient. But the two lines of argument, though often confused, are essentially distinct. Those who represent in the highest degree the spirit of tolerance are, as a rule, somewhat sceptical about the operations of self-interest; and those who lay most stress on the universal beneficence of self-interest are apt to reduce their belief in toleration to a theory rather than a practice.

We have thus far been considering the subject of liberty from the former of these two standpoints. We have shown how freedom of thought and action has been developed by civilized communities, under safeguards which look toward the use of that freedom for public purposes. Those who represent this view cherish no illusions as to the results of the freedom they advocate. They know that the exercise of freedom means mistakes; *"Es irrt der Mensch, so lang er strebt"*—Error is incident to every serious effort at human progress; but they see that these mistakes are relatively unimportant in comparison with the improvement which is attained if we allow them and prevented if we do not allow them. The doctrine of liberty, says Morley, rests on the belief that there are in the great seed plot of human nature a vast number of undeveloped germs, not tares and not wheat, whose properties we have not yet had a full chance to ascertain; and if you are over-anxious to pluck up the tares you pluck up these untried possibilities of human excellence, and are very likely to injure the growing wheat as well. Where this theory of toleration has taken root—and it has taken root to a greater or less extent among all the civilizations of modern Europe—there will be many acts which public sentiment judges harmful, but which it refrains from repressing because the evil of tyrannical interference outweighs the probable good to be gained; and there will be a vastly greater number of acts of which the community will not trouble itself to decide collectively whether the harm outweighs the good or not, because it prefers the slow process of experiment to any premature application of social judgment and administrative repression.

This system of toleration may be carried to such an extreme that it becomes a sort of political indifference. When it reaches this stage, it gives rise to an easy-going doctrine of political liberty which is as unhistorical as the doctrines of freedom of the will or of liberty of private judgment already alluded to—the so-called *laissez faire* doctrine that if you can only let people sufficiently alone matters will somehow work themselves out all right, and that the highest goal of jurisprudence is an organized policy of non-interference, where each individual's privacy is fully respected. But a far larger part of the advocacy of the policy of non-interference, especially in its extreme forms, comes from another quarter. It comes from men who are not content with tolerating the exercise of individual selfishness as harmless, but give it their positive approval as a means, and commonly a most effective means, to the attainment of the general good.

The conduct of the business of any civilized society involves the doing of a great many things which are unpleasant and disagreeable to the individuals involved. Society has at its command several agencies for making its individual members assume these necessary inconveniences and pains. It can rely on constraint, either physical or moral, on sympathy, or on self-interest. In the earlier stages of civilization it makes very large use of constraint. In all stages, early and late, sympathy is an important factor in securing the results desired. The systematic use of self-interest as a means to this end is of subsequent origin. But as time goes on and civilization advances, constraint falls into the background. In a thoroughly civilized community the physical penalties of the law are invoked only in exceptional instances, and the moral terrors are much mitigated. The fear of the anger of the gods gives place to the fear of public opinion; and for the majority of the citizens, this public opinion is based on views and sentiments which they themselves feel so strongly that its demands do not produce the feeling of constraint which they otherwise would. The precepts of such a public opinion fall in line with a man's own sympathies; so that in a really well developed community it is often impossible to draw any sharp line between the two and undertake to say where the motive of sympathy ceases and that of obedience to public opinion begins.

All this relaxation of constraint gives the individual more room to exercise choice as to his conduct, and makes it increasingly important to enlist his self-interest on the side of public service and social order. To a certain extent this is an easy thing to do. If a man has made any progress in civilization, his sympathies with his children are so strong that he will be sure of regarding their interests as his own, and will promote their welfare and enjoyment as an essential element in his personal gratification. What holds true of his dealings with his children is true, though to a less extent, of his dealings with his relatives and friends. Their pleasure is his pleasure; and even on grounds of mere selfishness he would not be likely to do that which would give them pain or do them harm, on account of the indirect distress to himself which would be caused thereby. Indeed, the same principle applies to his wider relations with the general public. The approbation of his fellow men has become so far a valuable object to him personally that he is not going to shirk inconveniences or run away from dangers if by so doing he will forfeit that approbation.

There have been many philosophers, both ancient and modern, who were disposed to base their theory of morals on the assumption of this identity of self-interest and public interest. *"Nihil honestum quod non idem utile"*—there is no moral good which cannot be proved advantageous to the individual—this was the theme which Cicero discussed in his De Officiis, and to which he gave a qualified assent. The same theme was discussed and the same qualified assent repeated by Herbert Spencer, in his Data of Ethics, nearly two thousand years afterward. The philosophers who hold this view of morals argue somewhat as follows: All our reasoning about conduct is based upon the assumption that an individual has a choice between different courses of action, and is to exercise his private judgment in preferring one to another. If he makes a choice and uses his reason, he is by the very necessities of the case bound to choose that course of conduct which he regards as more advantageous for himself. Of course this does not mean that he chooses that line whose advantages are more obvious. On the contrary, if he is at all intelligent, he will be led to give greater weight to remote ends than a less intelligent man would give, and will care more for the higher pleasures in comparison with the lower ones. He will lay less stress upon physical enjoyments, and more upon the pleasures of sympathy, of public approbation, and of that content which is found only in the approval of his own conscience. But after making all these explanations, the philosophers tell us the fact remains that calculated conduct is, in the very nature of the case, selfish conduct; and that under such circumstances the good, as distinct from the bad, represents the more enlightened and intelligent conduct, as distinct from the more shortsighted and self-destructive. The pursuit of physical pleasure speed-

FREEDOM AS A FOUNDATION OF ETHICS 109

ily brings satiety and pain. The pursuit of ease and cowardice brings public contempt. Therefore voluptuousness and cowardice are bad. The love of one's family and friends, the reward of social approbation, and best of all, the peace of mind which is engendered by a good conscience, are lasting pleasures, which have in them a depth which the voluptuary or the coward cannot understand. They therefore can be called good; and we can appeal to men to prefer them to shortsighted pleasure seeking on grounds of mere intelligence. Nay more; if we admit the fact of choice and the possibility of calculation, this is the only logical ground on which to make such an appeal.* Such was the reasoning of the Epicureans; such has been the reasoning of no small part of the philosophic students of ethics, whether in the ancient or the modern world.

But there is an obvious difficulty in this system

* This argument is sometimes carried to the extent of implying that every man is really actuated by considerations of his own happiness, even when he thinks he is working for others—that if he sacrifices himself for his friend, it is because he is so constituted that it gives him more pain to see his friend suffer than to put his own life in peril. But this line of reasoning involves a fallacy. It is true that a man always obeys the strongest motive; it is not true that strength of motive and quantity of happiness are the same thing. Strength of motive is matter of pure intensity; quantity of happiness involves intensity and duration both. If we believe that a certain course of conduct

of ethics which laid it open to criticism from the outset. Not all men, nor a majority of them, are of such intelligence as to render it safe for them to make their own happiness a conscious end or standard of right. The parallelism of a man's own selfish interests with those of the community, important as it sometimes may prove, is very incomplete except in the case of those men who have attained a high degree of advancement in civilization or excellence of personal character. There are unfortunately some people who abuse their children in order to give comfort to themselves, a still larger number who evade their obligations to their relatives for the sake of their own personal convenience, and an enormous number with whom the dictates of convenience or cowardice—if that cowardice is not going to be too prominently exposed—outweigh the love of social approbation. Under such circumstances, there is grave danger that conduct dictated

will give us happiness, this belief strengthens the intensity of our motive to choose that line of conduct; but the happiness is not the same thing as the motive, nor is it the only thing which determines the motive's intensity. If a man has much self-consciousness and little sympathy, his own future happiness will affect him intensely, and that of others but slightly; if he is less self-conscious and more sympathetic, other people's pleasure or pain, especially if visible, may cause far greater intensity of motive than does the prospect of his own future happiness or unhappiness.

by self-interest will be selfish in the bad sense of the word—will be used to promote the interests of the individual at the expense of those of the community.

In the face of this difficulty, ancient writers have held somewhat different views from modern ones. The ancient philosophers generally considered that free thought was to be the privilege of the few rather than the common heritage of the many. It was to be confined to those whose legal position was such that they could readily identify the interests of the body politic with their own, and whose intelligence was sufficient to make them prefer the higher and more permanent pleasures to the lower and more transient ones. The study of justice was to be the monopoly of an intellectual aristocracy. For the great bulk of the community, the *banausoi* or base mechanicals, it was necessary to preach the virtues of courage and self-restraint and sympathy —virtues which did not involve an exercise of the intellect; virtues which influenced choice in the direction of the public welfare, instead of emphasizing its character as an individual act of selfish reason.

This limitation of the freedom of choice, which seemed natural enough to the philosophers of the ancient world, has not been accepted in modern times. This is partly because our increasing democracy of intellect has led us to feel that a theory of morals which is good for anything must be couched in terms sufficiently general to let us preach it to everybody; but still more because the modern world has witnessed an extraordinary economic development in which the self-interest of individuals has actually been turned to the benefit of the community in unexpected ways. This economic history has been so striking that people have not only accepted its teachings, but exaggerated them. Self-interest in the industrial field has been made to do so much that many thinkers overestimate its benefits, and are quite prepared to extend it to other fields where its applicability is more doubtful. It has accomplished so much in one line that people are prone to believe that it would do everything that society needs, in that line and in all others, if it only had a fair chance.

The course of events in this industrial history may be summarized as follows:

Down to the close of the thirteenth century people looked to compulsion rather than to freedom— to public authority rather than to personal interest —as a means of getting the world's work done. Men were forced to labor by fear of the lash or the prison, instead of being encouraged to labor by the opportunity of bettering their social condition. Property right in these early days was essentially a military tenure, established for the sake of public security. People were given holdings of land in consideration of the service as soldiers which they had rendered or could render to the government. The land which they thus held these landholders did not till or improve. It was tilled for the most part by villeins, who, in return for the privilege of being allowed to occupy a part of the land, and call it in a measure their own, gave one-half of their time in compulsory labor for the military chieftain or feudal lord.

In the course of the thirteenth and fourteenth centuries, however, a large portion of the English villeins were allowed to substitute money payments for compulsory labor as a condition of holding their land. The immediate motive for this change was the need of the feudal lords for money; but its ultimate effect was a very great increase in the wealth of the country, public as well as private. Under the old system of compulsory labor the peasant had no motive to increase his production. He did as little as he could without being punished. Under the new system he had every motive to do as much as he could; for whatever he produced above the fixed money rent was a benefit to him individually. In other countries the change was not carried so far as in England. In Italy, for instance, the peasant, instead of paying the feudal lord a fixed money rent, generally agreed to pay him one-half of the produce. Thus he got only one-half the benefit of his increased activity, instead of the whole; and the effect in stimulating labor was but half as good as that of the English system. But in every European country, as far as the change was carried out, it increased the laborer's feeling of personal independence and his contribution to the public wealth.

For the benefit resulting from increased production did not stop with the first owner of the product. It distributed itself throughout the community. The accumulation of food supplies afforded a reserve on which the nation could fall back in time of war or famine or any other event which strained its economic resources. And when there was no war or famine the surplus could be used for paying men who were engaged in the work of agricultural improvement, in the development of machinery, in the building of shops, or in the production of poems and plays. The existence of capital made invention possible; and the chief benefit of these inventions went, not to the owner or investor of the capital, but to the public as a whole. The England of the

FREEDOM AS A FOUNDATION OF ETHICS 115

thirteenth century had been a country of unimproved farms, whose methods of production were rude and whose inhabitants lived from hand to mouth. The England of the eighteenth century was a country of highly improved land, with well developed industrial arts, producing much larger amounts both of food and of other things that made life worth living than it did five hundred years before. The chief thing that made the change possible was that system of industrial emancipation which gave men a selfish motive to work hard and to invest their capital in improvements. Of course this change was not unaccompanied with hardship. There were some men whose lot under the new system was worse than under the old; but of its good effect on the power and prosperity of the nation as a whole there can be no doubt whatever.

Neither the laborers nor the capitalists who contributed to this change were actuated by any philanthropic motive. They were trying to make all the money that they could. The significant thing is, that by letting them make all the money they could the community had helped instead of hindered its general prosperity. Selfishness had been made to contribute to the common good. In some commercial transactions the coincidence between individual selfishness and common good was so unexpected that the community had to reverse its old ethics completely. Take, for instance, the system of interest. In the thirteenth century this was universally condemned. Nothing could appear, at first sight, more avariciously selfish than the attempt to make a man who borrowed money of you pay back more than he had borrowed, simply because he was in present trouble and could not help himself. For this reason our forefathers called all interest by the opprobrious name of usury. The mediæval church condemned it as a sin; the mediæval courts punished it as a wrong. If you wanted any return on your money you were told to invest it yourself, and content yourself with profits actually earned. But the advantage to the community of having capital controlled by men who really knew how to manage it— by men who were progressive without being reckless—was so great that it was found desirable to encourage people to lend their money to such men instead of investing it themselves. The system of interest was a means of giving this encouragement. It allowed the lender, who had accumulated capital but had no special ability in managing it, to get the assurance of a moderate return; it allowed the borrower, who assumed the risk and responsibility of directing large business enterprises, to obtain the surplus gain which was due to his superior talent.

And, most important of all, it gave the community the chance to have its disposable stock of goods used in a way to produce the maximum of industrial progress.

But the most striking instance of the harmony between intelligent self-interest and public advantage was seen in connection with the sales and prices of goods.

The old theory of value was that every article had a just price; that the buyer would naturally try to pay less than that price, the seller to exact more; that whichever man succeeded gained a slight earthly advantage at corresponding peril to his soul—this peril being especially great in the case of the seller, because he was usually more skilful than the buyer and was likely to make this unfair gain a means of livelihood. For the double purpose of protecting the buyer against dangers in this life and the seller against dangers in the life to come, it was habitual for the authorities to fix prices on many of the articles of common use, and to exact severe penalties for any variation from these prices. If the authorities thought that a loaf of bread ought to cost two pence, they set the price accordingly and cut off the ears of the offending baker who should undertake to charge more. Of course the result of this was to fix the price at two pence. No baker was going to jeopardize his soul's salvation and his ears at the same time. The effect of this low price was that the consumers used bread as freely as before, instead of economizing it; and that after a few weeks, in place of the slight deficiency of supply which was tending to cause the increase in price, the community found itself face to face with an actual scarcity of the necessaries of life. The artificial system of price regulation had intensified the very evil that it was intended to prevent. A far wiser thing to do was to recognize that the high price was the symptom of an evil, rather than the cause of evil itself. If the baker was allowed to advance his price to two and a half pence, this in the first place caused economy of bread; and thus, by exercising a little care at the beginning, the community avoided the terrible evils of famine at the end. But this was not all. The advance of price to two and a half pence tended to attract supplies of wheat and flour from other communities where there had been no such scarcity. By refusing to allow any increase of price, you prevented people in other places from coming to your assistance. By allowing the increase you encouraged them to relieve the scarcity; so that after a brief period the price of bread in open market tended to return nearly to the former level. The high price was but

FREEDOM AS A FOUNDATION OF ETHICS

a symptom of a temporary or local scarcity. The man who attempted to lower the price by law was like the physician who should attempt to treat a disease by repressing its manifestations. The man who let things take care of themselves was dealing with the disease by the more enlightened method of providing natural means for the removal of its cause.

This experience with sales and prices was the basis of the principle of competition, which has taken such a hold on modern industrial life. If goods are scarce we let the buyers bid against one another; holding that by this process of selection we shall put such supplies as we have in the place where they are most urgently needed, and shall stimulate real economy in the use of the article by the temporary increase in its price. If the seller thus obtains a considerable gain, we regard this gain as fairly due to his forethought in providing the market with a supply of goods which would otherwise have been absent; and we interfere only when, by some combination or monopoly, he has produced an artificial scarcity instead of helping to meet one which already existed from natural causes. We believe also that the best remedy for a scarcity is to stimulate competition on the part of other producers who will devote their energies toward bringing new supplies to market; and who, if the scarcity is widespread or long continued, will invest new capital in the production of the goods thus urgently needed. We believe that the exceptional profit which these producers obtain until the deficiency of supply has been made good is but a natural and normal means of stimulating them to the utmost exertions in making good the deficiency and of rewarding them for their foresight in doing it rightly.

Thus the pursuit of self-interest is not always to be monopolized by the few, as the ancient philosophers supposed. These last two matters—interest and prices—were things where the ancient writers believed the exercise of selfishness most unsafe, and its results most destructive; and yet these are two cases where it does the clearest public good.

There can, I think, be no reasonable doubt that the world is far better served under this competitive system than under any other system of industrial regulation which has hitherto been tried. The effect has been so marked that modern law—the English first and the Continental afterward—has gradually adjusted itself to the conception that prices should be let alone wherever competition can regulate them; that a price obtained in open market, without fraud or artificial monopoly, is *ipso facto* a fair price; and that a man does no wrong to those with whom he deals if he buys as cheaply as he can and sells as dearly as he can. These legal principles have been reflected in our ethical conceptions. We assume that a competitive price is a morally just price; that what a man can obtain for an article in open market at the moment represents its present value; and that the average price which he can obtain in the long run represents its true or permanent value. We believe that under ordinary conditions the business man does his duty by the community if he observes the rules of the game of competition, as thus laid down; because by a general adoption of these rules the collective interest of the industrial community has been well served.

The strength of this theory of competition has been increased because of the fact that its opponents have rarely done it full justice. They have been so impressed by certain incidental evils connected with the system—smaller capitalists pushed to the wall by larger capitalists; intelligent workmen thrown out of employment by the process of industrial readjustment to make room for those cheaper and less skilled—that they have shut their eyes to its essential excellences. They have said that competition was nothing but a new name for the Darwinian struggle for existence as applied in modern business; that it was a glorification of the principle of survival of the strongest. This is a very imperfect view of the case. Competition is something essentially different in character from the struggle for existence among the lower animals. It is a struggle so ordered that outside parties reap a benefit, instead of suffering an injury. This is its conspicuous and distinctive feature. If cats are struggling to get the same bird, and bosses are struggling to get the same workmen, the relation of the cats to one another bears some analogy to the relation of the bosses to one another. But there is this radical difference in the whole transaction: that the more cats there are, the worse for the bird; while the more bosses there are, the better for the workmen. Competition is what its name implies—a concurrent *petition;* an effort on the part of different people to do the best they can for somebody else, in order to induce him to enter into dealings with them.

Unfortunately, it is not only the opponents of competition who fail to recognize this as its essential feature. The advocates of the system are prone to make a somewhat similar mistake. They apply the substantially sound theory that the value of a thing is what it will bring in open market to cases

FREEDOM AS A FOUNDATION OF ETHICS 123

where conception of open market is not accurate—sometimes because the market is not open, and sometimes because the thing is not marketable. They go so far as to assume that any adjustment which is the result of free play among a mixture of conflicting social elements, strong and weak, is presumably right, and should be interfered with only when the resulting evils are so clear as to furnish the most obvious grounds for state action. Starting from the theory—which is probably correct—that a business which pretends to be managed on better principles than those of self-interest usually turns out to be managed on worse principles, they draw the unwarranted conclusion that this same theory will hold true of other departments of life where the special conditions affecting business competition are absent. They permit self-interest to be the dominant guide in a man's public relations, and sometimes even in his personal relations also. They take the principle of the ancient philosophers, that the individual will be governed by selfish motives whenever he tries to calculate the results of his conduct; and, seeing that the application of this theory works out good results in commercial life, they conclude that we can find ways of making it bring out equally good results everywhere else. The account of rational egoism in Herbert Spencer's Data of Ethics may serve as a good example of this mental attitude. The author feels that the increasing exercise of enlightened selfishness is inevitable; and with this probability in view, he does all he can to prove it to be beneficial. Whatever may be thought of this book and its conclusions, there can be no doubt that it represents the attitude of a very large body of intelligent readers toward questions of practical and theoretical morality.

The modern world cannot accept the position of the ancient philosophers in treating egoism as a moral theory to be monopolized by a few highly educated philosophers or jurists. The world demands that whatever its theories are, they should be of a nature to be preached in the market place. If we claim that self-interest is a correct principle, we must give the people a chance to act on it and see what comes thereof. If evil and destruction come, it will prove that we must modify our statement of the theory. The actual everyday morality of each generation is determined by the degree of success which has attended the operation of principles which were tried experimentally by the generations immediately preceding. Down to about 1850 the complete extension of self-interest over the economic field and its partial extension into other fields produced an amount of good which far out-

FREEDOM AS A FOUNDATION OF ETHICS 125

weighed the incidental evil. Therefore the body of thinking men in the last generation was disposed to consider it an excellent theory to accept. Our experience of its further development in the last half of the nineteenth century has been more doubtful; and there is a corresponding doubt whether the next generations are going to accept individualistic theories as unreservedly as most men do today.

VI

THE LIMITS OF INDIVIDUAL FREEDOM

THE theory that individual selfishness could be trusted to promote the common good was so comfortable a doctrine that it found very strong prepossessions in its favor. Those who were solicitous for the common good were pleased to think that it could be attained by so easy a method. Those who believed that intelligent people were likely to be selfish whenever they reasoned concerning their conduct were glad to be assured that this practice would do good rather than harm to the public. Our experience during the first half of the nineteenth century seemed to justify the advocates of individualism in these optimistic hopes. Most of the restrictions upon trade which had been inherited from previous centuries were so bad that their removal paved the way for a better state of things. By giving each man liberty to choose the line of life which best suited him, we added to our industrial efficiency. By encouraging the investment of capital wherever any one saw a chance for profit,

LIMITS OF INDIVIDUAL FREEDOM 127

we stimulated invention and enabled the arts to develop as they had never done before. By allowing competition to regulate prices, we provided for better economy in the distribution of the world's products and for greater enjoyment in their consumption. There were indeed marked instances of evil in the midst of this general good. The abuse of labor, and particularly of child labor, under long hours and uncomfortable conditions of work required special legislation to suppress it. But on the whole, the evils incident to the change seemed so few and the advantages so many that people's minds dwelt upon the latter to the exclusion of the former. Under these circumstances, men were disposed to regard the principle of non-interference not as a principle of administration, but as a fundamental rule of social action; not as a maxim of experience, but as a postulate of thought.

This dogmatism in stating the principles of individual liberty, and this optimism in believing its results to be universally good, naturally provoked a reaction. About 1830 there arose a school of thought which cast doubt upon the economic advantage of the unrestricted liberty of each man to do as he pleased, and which set up a principle of socialism as opposed to that of individualism. These writers, scattered through France and Germany, emphasized the need of organized collective activity. That freedom which the advocates of non-interference regarded as the final stage in economic history was, to the members of this new school, only an intermediate step in the course of economic progress. Before the revolution of 1789, said Ferdinand Lassalle, one of the leaders of this new socialistic movement, Europe had solidarity without freedom. Since that date it has had freedom without solidarity. A third stage of evolution will combine the two, and give the poor man something more than the mere name of freedom, which under present conditions is little more than the assurance of being crushed to the wall.—The spread of these ideas was for the moment checked by the revolution of 1848, with which most of the leaders of European socialism were identified, and whose failure involved them in a certain measure of discredit. But after a brief interval ideas similar to those of Lassalle began to take root in many different quarters—among practical men as well as theorists, conservatives as well as agitators. The philanthropist demanded special laws to regulate factories in the public interest, because self-interest provided no remedy against excessive hours and did not prevent the use of methods of manufacture dangerous to life and health. The railroad manager was inclined to favor the principle of monopoly in industries like his own, because he saw the waste of capital and irregularity of organization which was consequent upon the building of parallel roads. The trades unionist was still more frankly in favor of regulations looking toward the monopoly of labor, both for his own special ends and for the sake of what he believed to be the good of the working classes as a whole. The protectionist, however much he might desire to see free competition within each country, made such sweeping exceptions to this principle in the trade between different countries as to weaken its hold upon the public mind; and it is well known that with the increase of national feeling among different countries in the last two generations there has been a great increase in the protectionist sentiment. And even those who were not greatly affected by any of these movements—who were neither reformers nor monopolists, trades unionists nor protectionists—have been forced to recognize that competition and non-interference act less perfectly than was once supposed, and must be applied with more reservations than some of our fathers assumed. Take for instance the point at which competition was supposed to work best—the regulation of prices. The price theory of Adam Smith and Ricardo was based upon the idea that if prices were unfairly low, producers could withdraw from business until the supply was so reduced that the price returned to a remunerative level; and conversely, that if prices were too high, new producers could enter into competition until the supply was increased and the rate of profit reduced to a reasonable figure. But in industries requiring large permanent investment neither of these conditions is realized. If the supply of products from a certain factory is inadequate to meet the demand for its goods, we must wait months before we can expect to have relief from a competing factory; if the supply of transportation over a certain railroad is inadequate to meet the demand for its services, we must wait years before relief can be reached by a competing railroad. If, on the other hand, prices are too low, it is almost impossible for a factory or a railroad already existing to withdraw from competition. The capital remains, whether business goes on or not. It involves worse loss to let it go wholly to waste than to sell goods or services below cost. Under conditions like these we see great fluctuations in rates, which competition is powerless to prevent.

Nay, such competition as there is tends to increase these fluctuations by the irregular and spasmodic character of its action. If it acts at some places and not at others we have discrimination, usually in favor of the large city and against the country town or farming locality—a thing which intensifies the dangerous drift toward the large cities which is characteristic of recent years. If it acts at some times and not at others, we have those alternations between periods of high price and low price which form one of the most unfortunate features in a commercial crisis. Such spasmodic competition is fierce while it lasts, and it has the effect of teaching the different competitors to exert themselves to the utmost to meet the needs of the public. But it does not have the effect of steadying prices, nor ensuring equal treatment to the different consumers. It has retained its force as a stimulus; it has lost its force as a regulator of charges.

But there are many lines in which even this partial and imperfect competition is becoming a thing of the past. In some forms of business the masses of capital needed for the successful use of modern inventions are so large that this fact of itself creates a monopoly. In others, the evils arising from the irregular and spasmodic competition just described are so serious that different persons engaged in the same line of business arrange to form a monopoly, by the consolidation, virtual or actual, of all the competing concerns. When this result has been brought about, the social machinery on which our fathers relied for securing fair prices has fallen to the ground. It may be that the new mechanism which has come in its place will ultimately prove as good as the old; but it is, at any rate, wholly different in character. Where we had competing concerns engaged in supplying the market, the consumer was immediately and directly protected by the fact that if one man did not serve him properly he could go to another; and the knowledge that the consumer had this resource compelled the several competitors to consult his interests rather than their own. Where consolidation has been brought about, there is no such immediate protection. The producer knows that the consumer has no other equally good source of supply to which he can go, and this fact makes a difference in his whole mental attitude and that of his agents. He may be, and in the case of our best leaders of industry probably will be, anxious to do what the public really needs and do it well. He will feel that his interests, in the long run, cannot be different from those of the public; that the size of his investment of capital makes a large market imperative; that this large market can be secured only by a system of low prices; and that the economy which results from his improvements in machinery and organization must therefore be used for the benefit of the public, in order that it may prove in the long run to be any economy at all. Of our large industrial monopolies some, including the most successful ones, have been managed with this principle in view. But there are others which have not been thus managed—whose directors have been more concerned to keep prices high than to increase their volume of traffic, and have tried to retain a large share of the benefits of their economy for themselves and give only a small share to the public. A large number of men who have been charged with the management of consolidated industries, and a still larger number of their subordinate agents, have assumed that it was right for them to consult their own immediate interests under a system of monopoly as freely as they would have done under the old system of competition. They have not realized that the widening power, both for good and for evil, which was given them by their new positions rendered it imperatively necessary for them to take a wider view of their duties and obligations to the public than was needed under the old system, and to apply the principle of self-interest with more circumspection than was necessary in previous generations.

The danger to the consumer which is incident to

our present industrial conditions is most clearly illustrated when we have two monopolies in conflict with one another, blocking the public service for their own strategic ends. Two opposing railroads in the same territory, for instance, will arrange their trains so that they do not connect with one another—each being more concerned with injuring its rival than with meeting the wishes of the travelling public. Here we see a Darwinian struggle for supremacy, with little or nothing of that service to third parties which is the essential feature in the competitive system. The most marked cases of this kind occur in connection with those large strikes when a monopoly of labor on the one side is arrayed against a monopoly of capital on the other. The telegraph service was thus interrupted in 1883. The railroad transportation of large sections of the community was tied up in 1877 and 1886 and 1894. In 1902 the whole production of anthracite coal was brought practically to a standstill in one of these conflicts, with no regard to the interests of the consumers, and with great suffering to many of them.

I shall not at this moment inquire into the relative merits of the case of the coal companies on the one hand or of the men on the other. We are not concerned with awarding praise or blame to the parties in dispute. We are concerned with a much broader question—the question of awarding praise or blame to society for its economic system. We are being called upon to decide whether the operation of individual self-interest is a safe agency for ensuring public service and meeting public necessities. In this case we find that it was not. We look in vain in the records of either side of the anthracite coal controversy for any recognition of the special obligation of the coal producers to supply the public with a sufficient quantity of coal which was incident to their character as monopolies of capital and labor, if monopolies of capital and labor were to be allowed to exist at all. Both parties to the controversy claimed the right to do everything which they could properly have done if competition had existed. Of intelligent preparation to have adequate supplies in the hands of the consumers there was very little indeed. The operators, instead of encouraging the importation of coal from abroad at an early period, in order to forestall the market's needs, kept saying up to the very last moment that the strike was on the point of coming to its end. The unions, instead of treating the public distress as something for which they were at least partly responsible, seemed chiefly concerned to aggravate it as a means of putting greater pressure upon the authorities to intervene. The breaches of the obligation of contract that did occur, and the threat, happily unfulfilled, of a monumental breach of contract by a sympathetic strike in the bituminous coal regions, show clearly the unfitness of many of the persons concerned to be relieved from the industrial control of competition, until some other means of control has been provided in its stead. The principle of self-interest conspicuously failed to protect the public in the anthracite coal strike. We may expect recurrent failures of this sort unless we can either modify our industrial conditions or our principles of ethics.

Can we thus modify the industrial conditions?

Among the many means which have been suggested for doing this, three deserve special attention: First, an extension of the system of contracts between companies and their operatives, so that incorporated capital shall deal with incorporated labor in a responsible fashion. Second, an extension of the conspiracy laws so that combinations adverse to the interest of the consumers as a body can be treated as criminal and suppressed by the organized force of the community. Third, an extension of the principle of direct government management—the so-called socialistic principle—to those industries where continuous production or continuous service is a matter of vital public necessity.

LIMITS OF INDIVIDUAL FREEDOM 137

The extension of the system of long-time contracts, with proper arrangements for arbitration in case of misunderstanding, is on its face the simplest of these three remedies. If we could assume that such a contract would be kept when once made, and that the decision of such a board of arbitration, when once established, would meet cheerful acquiescence, no better solution could be devised. But we are far from being able to make that assumption. It will be remembered that some of the mines which were closed in the recent coal strike already had in operation such a system of contracts, and that these agreements were broken by the laborers. To give us a really effective system of contract and arbitration, one of two things must happen. Either we must have a rigid law compelling all labor unions to be incorporated, and requiring them to furnish adequate security for the performance of their contracts; or we must educate the laborers themselves to a higher sense of the obligation of contract and the necessity of carrying it out, even to their own apparent disadvantage.

Each of these alternatives involves us in some difficulty. If we deny the right of unincorporated bodies of laborers to make collective bargains for their work, we take away a great deal of liberty which already exists; and this process is always an exceedingly difficult one. We are not situated as we should be if our labor had previously been compulsory and we now, as a concession in the direction of freedom, allowed the laborers to make contracts if they could furnish pecuniary security for their performance. Having once left them free to make these bargains without the restriction, it is going to be very difficult to reimpose it by statute. It is almost equally hard, under the circumstances, to add sacredness to the labor contract in the mind of the workman himself. A contract for wages connected with future service deals with economic conditions which shift very rapidly, and afford continual grounds for demanding readjustment. Sometimes these readjustments are of a kind where the reasons for the arbitrators' award are clear; sometimes they are not. If we have taught the workman by precept and example that it is his economic right and duty to look out for himself, there is very grave danger that under any system of arbitration, however carefully guarded, he will find sufficient pretext to justify himself in his own mind for disregarding the award. Only as part of a general movement toward increased sacredness of obligations to others, and diminished sacredness of the obligations of self-interest, can we expect to see any considerable reform in the work-

LIMITS OF INDIVIDUAL FREEDOM 139

man's conception of his duties under wage contracts for the future.

The second means proposed for preventing the recurrence of difficulties like the anthracite coal strike is a stricter definition of the laws of conspiracy. But here we are met by the inquiry, Which is the conspirator? The workman considers the combination of mine owners as an attempt to establish a monopoly to the detriment of the welfare of the state, and regards the efforts of his union to organize the laborers as being at the very worst a legitimate effort to fight fire with fire. The representatives of the corporations, on the other hand, see in their own organizations responsible creatures of the law, working under legal forms; while the union is to them an intruder, a counter-organization without equal historical or legal standing, arranged for the purpose of producing artificial scarcity of labor. Each party is so occupied beholding motes in its brother's eye that it is unable to see the beam which is in its own eye, or to take any steps for plucking it out. I very gravely doubt the possibility, under ordinary conditions, of bringing home either to trades unions or to industrial corporations the guilt of conspiracy against the public. For as long as the public recognizes self-interest as a dominant motive, to be pursued to the exclusion of other motives, so long will it look with toleration on combined or organized acts of self-interest, and will resent any demand to punish as criminal conspiracies the organizations which perpetrate them.

It is not indeed difficult to formulate a theory of the law of conspiracy which will allow us to regard certain actions, which would be innocent and proper if they came separately, as being wrong when done in concert. Stanley Jevons, in his book on The State in Relation to Labor, gives a good illustration of this distinction. For a man to walk through the streets of one of our large cities is a perfectly innocent act. The street is provided for this very purpose. But if ten thousand men preconcertedly walk through a certain section of the street at the same hour it becomes a public nuisance; and if they have arranged this action with a view of obstructing traffic it becomes an offence against the law. Nevertheless it is noticeable that the courts and the police are reluctant to interfere with such crowds if they can possibly avoid it; and as for punishing individual men who are concerned in the manifestation, or trying to make them walk elsewhere, it often seems to transcend the power of the state. It can be done in monarchies, but at the cost of great unrest. In democracies it can hardly be done at all; for we are very reluctant to punish men for a thing in groups which we do not consider bad when done by individuals.

Any real reform in conspiracy law must come from a new conception of public responsibility. The readiness, either on the part of capitalist or laborer, to sacrifice the consumers' interests to his own, is itself morally bad. The prevalence of competition has permitted this truth to fall into the background, because it prevents the development of this evil possibility among persons of ordinary intelligence. Combination permits and encourages the evil, unless those who control the combination are more clear-headed than the average of mankind. Taking business as we find it, and human intelligence as we find it, we need some new standards of business morals in order to prevent industrial monopoly from degenerating into industrial conspiracy. If we stop short of this higher conception of industrial responsibility, and continue to hold to the idea of self-interest as a paramount industrial good, we cannot effectively deal with the abuses of monopoly, because we shall be simply attempting to punish someone else for doing effectively on a large scale what we, on our own part, have been trying to do much less effectively on a small one. But if we can really go to the root of the matter by changing our standards, we can establish a theory of conspiracy which we shall not be afraid to put to the test of practice.

The third means suggested to avoid the recurrence of dangers like that of the anthracite coal strike is the direct control and operation of productive industry by the government—in other words, a system of socialism.

This would doubtless modify very greatly the form which our conflicts would take; but it is by no means easy to prove that these conflicts would be wholly avoided thereby. Indeed, with democracies managed as they are at present, where one district is pitted against another, each seeking its own sectional interests; or where president stands on one side and congressman on another, each ready to face the dangers of a deadlock for the sake of the policy which he and those behind him represent; the danger of disregard of public needs in the pursuit of private interests would be increased rather than diminished.* The more intelligent among the

* A failure to act responsibly in handling a public corporation is not brought home to the managers as directly as a similar failure is brought home in the case of an ordinary private corporation or of an incorporated labor organization. When a socialistic experiment fails, the leader may be in some degree discredited; but the loss is so distributed over the whole body of the taxpayers, some of whom are probably the very ones who opposed the experiment from the first and are least responsible

LIMITS OF INDIVIDUAL FREEDOM

socialists recognize the danger of this sort of deadlock and conflict as government is managed at present; and they say that one of the benefits which they seek in giving additional powers to government is that it will compel people, in mere self-defence, to be more accurate in watching the details of its management. But the difficulty of exercising effective oversight under such conditions is very great indeed; and the chance for an outside observer to secure protection to public interests is even smaller than at present. For under present conditions the state comes in as an independent authority and checks the property owners if they go too far; but under a socialistic system, if once a ring came into power it would control politics and industry alike, and there would be no outside means of checking it except through the agency of revolution. If we grant that a socialistic state is managed by citizens who subordinate their own interests to the common interest, and hold their power as a public trust, most of the evils under which we now suffer would

for its failure, that the lesson is not brought home as it should be. In fact, there is danger that the distribution of these burdens on the responsible and irresponsible alike will teach exactly the wrong lesson, and lead people to think that power and freedom are privileges to be grasped by those who can get them, rather than trusts to be administered by those who can furnish the community security for their responsible exercise.

be avoided. But so they would under the present conditions of capitalistic enterprise if we had this habitual exercise of public spirit and recognition of public obligation. Without this spirit neither the restraint of conspiracy law nor the application of public ownership will go to the heart of the difficulty. So far as the development of private property helps to make people recognize public obligations, it is a good thing. So far as the extension of a system of contracts to labor disputes can help it, it will be a good thing. And, so far as socialism can help it, socialism will be a good thing. But modern socialism tends to get at this matter from the wrong end. It relies too much on mere machinery and too little on the force which is behind it. It is an attempt to use collective power for individual happiness, when what we want is an attempt to enlist individual power in the interest of collective happiness.

It seems as if a man's preferences between individualism and socialism were generally determined not on the basis of principle but on the basis of personal interest. His opinion on matters like public control and ownership of corporations is not so much influenced by an intelligent study of the relative effect of these two methods upon public service and public convenience as upon the basis of its relation to his own industrial power. If he is a rich man, and controls more money than votes, he is likely to be in favor of private management. If he is a poor man, and controls relatively more votes than money, he is likely to be in favor of public action. He prefers the form which gives to him individually, and to those situated like him, relatively greater means of making their voices heard, without having taken the trouble to assure himself that the things which he and his friends can say will really contribute to the best interests of the community.

It has been one of the unfortunate results of the industrial progress of the nineteenth century that our standards of public morals have been, so to speak, commercialized,—that we value things on a money basis, whether they are of a kind that ought to be bought and sold or not, and measure a man's position not by service which he has been able to do his fellow men so much as by the extent to which he has been able to compel them to render him a return. I am afraid that nine-tenths of the world rates the inventor or scientific discoverer who has rendered a public service lower than the patentee who has succeeded in making the public pay him for it. And this character of our standards would not be essentially altered by the transfer of industry to the hands of government officials, as some of the socialists think. We should be measuring a man's value by his control of votes instead of his control of dollars. So long as this spirit prevails we shall be subject in an extreme form to those political dangers described in the first lecture. We shall see government take the shape of organized efforts to use the resources of the community as a whole for the interest of some larger or smaller part thereof. We shall see the spirit of trusteeship sink into abeyance, and be replaced by the spirit of appropriation for selfish or local or short-sighted ends. While these standards prevail and these conditions last, it seems difficult to expect any real preventive of disastrous internal conflict. Each new complexity in our organization of industry, and each extension of the functions of government which puts the individual into contact with his fellows at more points than he had a generation ago, simply intensifies the evil and necessitates some really radical step toward its cure. In industry and in politics alike we must get back to the conception of some higher motive than self-interest and some better measure of value than self-aggrandizement.

Man, as Aristotle has well said, is a political animal. His power of forming communities, in

LIMITS OF INDIVIDUAL FREEDOM 147

which the individual shall be subordinated to the interests of the group, is one of his most distinctive qualities. His power of forming free communities, in which each individual shall by his own judgment direct his efforts to a public end, is a characteristic yet more distinctive; and this form of social organization gives him his greatest strength. But if self-government is not used enough to promote the resources of a community as a whole, but to divert those resources into individual channels, it becomes a source of weakness instead of strength—whether that weakness come in the form of enervation, as in Greece and Italy, or of incapacity for discipline, as in Poland, or of ambition and misdirected organization, as in France under the old regime.

We have traced step by step the lesson that freedom, moral, civil, religious, or industrial, is successfully given only in connection with the assumption of responsibility. It is for us to see that this present counter-current in the stream of our progress, which leads some to claim the privileges of freedom without assuming its responsibilities, be only momentary; and to insist on the duty of American citizens to accept the lessons of history and the responsibilities of freedom. If the thinking men of the country really take this view of the matter and carry it out even when it works to their own burden and detriment, the unthinking men will follow. There are fashions in reasoning, as well as in everything else; and those who can take the lead are given the lead. If they neglect this opportunity to give the right direction to thought, theirs will be the responsibility for the succession of political failures which must ensue. But if they insist, for themselves first, and by their example for others, that freedom shall be prized as a means of public service; that wealth shall be valued, and valued only, as an indication of services performed in the past and of the power to do similar service in the future; that public office is a public trust for the same end; then, and not till then, may we claim for our American democracy the merit of having solved, so far as human foresight can see, the problem of combining the liberty of the individual with the promotion of the public good.

In the centuries immediately past we have had to deal with the problem of securing liberty. Today we have to face the problem of preserving it. It is a great mistake to assume that the problem of today is the easier of the two. The hardships and dangers connected with it are less tangible; but they are on that account all the more difficult to assume. We no longer have to face the peril of the scaffold or the privation of the revolutionary camp; but we

LIMITS OF INDIVIDUAL FREEDOM

have to face and accept the peril and privation of imposing upon ourselves standards of conduct higher and duties more burdensome than those which we have hitherto recognized either in law or morals. Freedom has always required the exercise of courage to defend it from the assaults of its adversaries. It today requires the exercise of public spirit and personal self-restraint to guard against the excesses of those who deem themselves to be its friends. Only by the acceptance of this widened sense of responsibility and by the growth of this public spirit can we hope that the freedom, so laboriously wrought out in the centuries past, may be successfully preserved through those to come.

VII

THE OUTLOOK FOR THE FUTURE.

FOR the successful conduct of the affairs of a free people two things are necessary: an organization which enables each man to use his powers for the benefit of himself and his fellows with only the minimum of necessary interference; and a spirit among the individual members of the community which will lead them to take the responsibility which goes with this method of organization, and to make good use of it.

Each of these things is important in its way, but the second is the one which we need to watch more closely. The machine and the force that drives it are both essential to the doing of work; but a bad machine with plenty of power will usually accomplish better results than a good machine with inadequate power. If there is a proper spirit of political responsibility, defects in the social organization will be made good. If there is not this spirit on the part of the citizens, no machinery, however well devised, can be trusted to run continuously.

THE OUTLOOK FOR THE FUTURE 151

A few years ago the agent of a manufacturing company received a visit from a man who desired to buy a pump which should provide for the watering of his stock. When the agent inquired where he was to get the power to drive the machine, the visitor replied that he proposed to put in an instrument large enough to pump not only the water which he needed for his cattle, but an additional supply sufficient to run the machine itself. When he was told that this was impossible he expressed great disappointment. "It seems as though you ought to be able to do this for me," he said. "I am prepared to put a good deal of capital into this machine." We smile at the simplicity of a man who makes such a demand on our mechanicians; and yet it is paralleled every day in the writings and teachings of social reformers. They have a feeling that if the political mechanism were only good enough it would relieve them of the responsibility of running it—would, in short, furnish its own power. This misconception is not confined to professional reformers. It is reflected in the mental attitude of a large part of our citizens. They think that it is the business of constitutional lawyers to devise a government which shall give us the utmost freedom, and at the same time reduce our share in the actual work of running it to a minimum. They not only tolerate but encourage the use in our schools of text-books on civics which lay stress on the description of administrative details, and say almost nothing of the force of public opinion—which tell much of the methods of voting and the organization of legislative assemblies, but give no hint of the fact that a voter must be prepared to subordinate his own interests to those of the body politic, and a legislator to prefer the good of the country to the good of his district, if our republic is to continue a really free state. We are losing sight of the lessons of history as it used to be taught in the old-fashioned days. There is an appreciable danger that modern methods in the study of politics will give us little of what we need to learn concerning the real spirit which makes nations great.

As far as the mechanism of our social organization goes, we have no reason to complain of our lot. The family, the church, the school, not to speak of other less important agencies, provide for the development of sound personal relations. The complex agencies for the production and sale of goods—the market, the exchanges, and the banking system—provide the necessary framework for our industrial relations. Government, local, state, and national, in its various branches provides a means for the

THE OUTLOOK FOR THE FUTURE 153

ordering of our political relations. We may at times have occasion to complain of the way in which the different parts of this mechanism work. One man thinks that the teaching in the schools is bad; another complains that the banks do not furnish an elastic currency; a third criticises the rules which govern the action of the United States Congress. But these are mere details—unimportant defects in a complex piece of machinery which is the product of ages of experience, and which is on the whole well adapted to the work in hand. Let us turn our attention to that more important part of our inquiry which deals, not with the character of the machine, but with the way in which it is managed. Let us inquire in what spirit and by what power we, as individual citizens, undertake to operate this vast social organization. It is devised to give us the power of governing ourselves. Do we take the opportunity which it gives us, and actually exercise the privilege of self-government in a way to preserve, instead of jeopardizing, this social structure?

So far as concerns our personal relations, it can be safely said that we do. In our dealings with our families, our relatives, and our friends, we use our freedom not for the sake of self-aggrandizement, but as a means of giving pleasure to those about us.

We have learned to restrain our passions, not because somebody else compels us to, but as a matter of courtesy and self-respect. We have learned to consult others' happiness, not on grounds of calculation but on grounds of affection. We have trained ourselves, and have by our example been able to train others, in a system of personal morality where murder and robbery are almost unknown and where on an increasing scale chastity takes the place of license, courtesy moderates passion, and friendly devotion overcomes the temptations of indolence. Amid changes of religious belief we have preserved these habits, not only undiminished but actually increased; so that these parts of our morality no longer require the supernatural terrors of religion to enforce them, but are cheerfully assumed as voluntary duties toward our fellow men, in which the fear of future punishment counts for no more than the fear of the policeman. There are, indeed, points at which our personal morality is subject to a certain degree of danger. The increasing laxity of divorce, for instance, is thought by some to menace that acceptance of personal responsibility for the training of children which the old-fashioned view of the marriage contract so properly emphasized. But after making all possible exceptions, it is fair to say that in this twentieth century men and wom-

THE OUTLOOK FOR THE FUTURE 155

en in their personal relations assume a full measure of that responsibility which is necessary to the exercise of freedom.

In industrial relations the case is different. In those things which people regard as matters of business, the community relies on self-interest to take the place of self-government. Of course we do not carry this pursuit of self-interest to a point where it would violate our code of personal morality. We do not tolerate the ordinary and commonplace forms of lying and cheating. We do not use our commercial power to oppress individuals whom we know. We do not commit serious breaches of trust where the interests of some specific person have been placed in our charge. Commercial society would not tolerate any of these things; and even if it did, our own instincts of personal morality would prevent us from doing them. But when the personal relation does not come so prominently into the foreground; when the people who are injured by our conduct are not certain definite persons whom we see, but an unknown and indefinite body which we do not see; when we lay our plans to deceive, not some specific individual or group of individuals, but large sections of the public; when the trust which we are exercising, and which we have it in our power to break, is not in the name of some specific ward, but on behalf of a general body of stockholders or bondholders—then our standards are much less satisfactory. Many a man who would despise a grocer for using false measures in selling commodities will himself use false measure in selling securities. He deems it wrong to water milk, and right to water stock. He will not deceive an individual, but he has no scruples about deceiving the investing public. Nor are the men who indulge in those practices to be so severely blamed as would appear at first sight. If you could properly bring the blame home to the men you could stop the practice; for no man who is ambitious for real leadership in a community is going to do things which the conscience of that community can condemn. The blame rests upon the people as a whole. The commercial public has seen so much good arising from competition that it has come to rely upon this as a means of checking the evil effects of individual selfishness, and to regard it as far more powerful and universal than it really is. It has come to consider business as a game, to be played by each man in his own interest, subject to certain well defined rules or conventions of business life, but involving no special obligations outside of those rules. The public has assumed that if each man played this game fairly, with a view to secur-

THE OUTLOOK FOR THE FUTURE 157

ing all he could for himself, the general interests of industry and commerce would be well subserved.

We are, I think, beginning to be dissatisfied with this view of commercial ethics; and I regard this growing dissatisfaction as one of the most fortunate signs of the times. We are beginning to recognize that it is not enough to insist that the game of business should be played fairly, or to modify the ethics of that play by personal sentiment in those cases where we see the individual injury done, and those alone. We are recognizing that business is something more than a game which each man can play to win. In its modern shape commercial business for all its leaders represents a trust. I do not, of course, mean that it has become subject to that particular form of consolidation which the name trust at first sight suggests. Some of our corporate business is of that form; a far larger part is not. But, whatever be its external form or arrangement, its essential character is that the interests of a great number of people are entrusted to the hands of a president and board of directors. Upon the sagacity of this president and these directors depends the prosperity of hundreds of investors, thousands of operatives, and perhaps millions of consumers. If these men manage that trust primarily for their own interests, instead of for the interests of those whom they represent, it always results in evil, and sometimes in disaster. We cannot rely upon competition to prevent these consequences. Where it acts regularly and smoothly it may do a great deal toward preventing them; but the cases where competition acts smoothly and regularly are the exception rather than the rule in the large industries of the present day. Nor will the law reach these evils—at least until the community has modified its moral conceptions as well as its legal ones. A law which attempts to do more than the moral sense of the community really desires, and which undertakes to punish corporations for doing on a large scale things which people tolerate when done on a smaller scale, will inevitably become a dead letter.

One essential feature of a trust is that those to whom it is given have a discretionary power for good or evil. The law cannot prescribe exactly what they shall do and punish all deviations from the lines thus prescribed. It leaves them free to use their power well or ill, subject to the control of their own consciences and the moral sense of the community. In this sense modern industrial combinations are most clearly trusts. The means of providing for their proper exercise are moral ones.

THE OUTLOOK FOR THE FUTURE 159

The force of public opinion is the one really effective agency in this matter.

The improvement in the relations of directors to investors which was effected in the course of the nineteenth century was not primarily nor chiefly due to changes in the statutes. It was due to changes of public opinion in the business world. These changes started from men who were not always the wealthiest, but whose reputation and character enabled them to impose upon others whatever standards they voluntarily enforced upon themselves. Men do not as a rule desire money for its own sake. They desire it for the sake of the consideration which it brings. If the making of money by questionable methods causes them to receive less consideration than they otherwise would from people whose judgment they respect, they will abandon those methods.

The reforms in the relations of directors to the public represent only a beginning of what we need; but the fact that a beginning has been made shows that we have means of reform at command, if only we will use them. There are indications that we are going to use them more than we have done hitherto. There are signs of a demand for an increased recognition of the principle of trusteeship in the handling of wealth. Those events which for the moment seem most disastrous—fluctuations in the value of investments, and strikes which involve stoppage of production and commerce—bring home to the people the fact that our industrial system does not serve society as well as we supposed; that if these things grow much worse the time may come when it will be put on trial for its life; and that we must seriously set to work toward its betterment. Of course nine-tenths of the schemes proposed for such betterment are impracticable, or worse. The men who are most ready to suggest panaceas are usually the ones who know least of the difficulties of the case. But we have it in our power to carry out a slow but thorough reform of industrial relations if we simply keep this conception in view: that the amount of money made in business does not represent the real measure of a man's business power or business achievement. Our ethical standards in recent years have led us to place too high a valuation upon success in money-making as a test of a man's commercial and industrial efficiency. Money, after all, is but a tool of trade. It is an important means of service to society; and its possession or control may be important evidence that a man has rendered such service. But if we regard money as an end instead of a means, or confound the evidence of success with the success itself, we have made a most serious mistake in the arrangement of our standards. If a man gets money in ways which prove injurious to society instead of beneficial, this furnishes no more reason for giving him social consideration than it does in the case of the burglar or forger who has managed to escape state's prison by a technicality of the law. If men of good character, business sense, and clear-headed ethics can insist upon the duty of rendering continuous service to the public at reasonable rates, and by methods which prevent disastrous fluctuations in the value of securities, and regard wealth which is made by a sacrifice of these standards as prima facie evidence of moral weakness rather than of industrial power, the problem will be solved. I believe that there is no other way to its solution; and that in the present temper of the American people and the present power of public opinion, there is a very strong hope of making progress toward a solution on the lines here suggested.

Passing from industry to politics, we still find the same tendency to rely on self-interest—not so openly, perhaps, as in industrial life, but to a degree which involves the community in very considerable danger. Our system of commercial ethics has had a strong effect on our system of political ethics. I suspect that in ordinary times voters, so far as they do any thinking at all, are guided by personal considerations more than by public ones—especially when matters are under discussion which are not party measures. And what is true of voters is true of their representatives. The congressman is more closely busied about the interests of his district than about the interests of the public at large. Indeed, he will tell you frankly that when every other congressman is pushing the claims of his locality and his friends, it would cause confusion rather than advantage if he alone should sacrifice local and personal interests for those of the commonwealth. He would be in such a hopeless minority that he could accomplish little for the nation as a whole, and would simply prevent his constituents from getting an equitable share of the benefits of government. Where voters and their representatives are actuated by considerations like these, it is inevitable that politics should be regarded as a game in the same sense that business is regarded as a game. It will be characterized by effort on the part of individuals to advance their own interests, in the complacent belief that somehow or other, in the general scramble of a large number of men working in different directions, no great unfairness can result in the long run. I do not mean that this theory is as

THE OUTLOOK FOR THE FUTURE 163

universally accepted in politics as it has been in business. A large number of men go into politics with the intent of serving the public first, their friends next, and themselves, in any selfish fashion, not at all. But, with general conditions and general standards of political ethics as they exist at present, the difficulty of living up to this conception is very great.

In all these matters the analogy between industrial and political ethics is very close indeed. In our industrial ethics, we have come to regard the making of money as the test of power and the object of ambition. In our political ethics we regard the control of votes and the offices which they bring as furnishing a similar test. When once this standard is accepted, and this conception of politics as a game becomes universal, there is a tendency even on the part of the best men to look with leniency on all means tolerated by the rules of the game for securing votes necessary to nominate and elect a man to office; and to regard as quixotic the views of those who insist on the moral duty of sacrificing votes for the sake of convictions. It is not the office-seekers who are primarily to blame, but the community as a whole, because its general system of political ethics makes it difficult for a good man to pursue high standards without sacrificing his chances for political efficiency.

We see a great many attempts to meet this evil by superficial remedies. Some persons believe that much can be accomplished by independent voting. They say that if there is a group of electors who, instead of being attached to a particular party, will vote for the candidates who represent higher principles and better methods, politicians will be compelled to advocate good measures and nominate good officers. The men who hold this view are trying to apply the principle of competition to political affairs. They would let the persons who desire to hold office compete for the votes of those who do not. In local affairs this habit of non-partisan voting has become far more general than it once was, and has on the whole had distinctly good effects. "We are occasionally compelled to pander to the moral sense of the community," said an old-time politician, regretfully, as he surveyed the figures of an independent vote at a local election. But the importance of parties in the actual work of government in the United States renders it difficult to adopt a theory of politics which places the most intelligent and independent voters outside of the framework of party organization, and thus for the sake of an occasional influence at elections deprives them of the continuous influence within the councils of the party which they ought to have, and otherwise would have.

Another remedy proposed is exactly the reverse of this. It is suggested that there should be a greater participation of good men in the direct business of politics. It is urged that the men who have an interest in good government are more numerous than those who have an interest in bad government, and that it is the fault of these men if they do not make their influence felt. To a certain extent this point is well taken. Readiness on the part of disinterested men to accept the burdens of public service is always salutary. But until we get some better conceptions of political ethics than we now have, the amount which can be accomplished in this way is small in proportion to the magnitude of the effort. Where politics is a game, those who make it their life work to play the game, even if they be few in number, have the overwhelming advantage which the professional always has in dealing with the amateur. A great number of men giving a portion of their time to any game can scarcely deal on equal terms with a few men who give their whole time to the acquisition of special skill. When the pessimist was told, by way of encouragement, that God was stronger than the devil, he replied sadly that the devil made up for his inferior strength by his superior activity. This sort of obstacle stands in the way of the efforts of our Good Government Clubs and Citizens' Leagues, when they attempt to meet the professional politician on his own ground. To be permanently successful, the general body of citizens must fight on the ground where they are strongest; using public opinion as their weapon, and so shaping that public opinion that men will honor the politician not for the offices which he gets but for the responsibilities which he assumes. In politics, as well as in industry, we must substitute the conception of a trust for that of a game.

There are signs that this change of public sentiment is taking place. The acquisition of dependencies has emphasized, as nothing else could do, the importance of the theory that public office is a public trust. When we were occupied with the government of our own states and cities, appointment of bad men to office, though it might cause loss and waste, was not likely to produce wholesale spoliation and oppression. But when we came to deal with the inhabitants of the West Indies or the Philippine Islands, who had neither the constitutional guarantees nor the habits of political independence which would have protected them, it became obviously and imperatively necessary to have the right men in command. The government of the Philippine Islands could not be treated as a game. It was bound to be either a trust or a scandal. When our dealings with dependent races had been on a small scale and in our own back yard, as in the case of the Indians, we had not infrequently allowed them to become scandals. But with our assumption of new and large responsibilities in the sight of the whole world it became a matter both of pride and of necessity to treat government of dependencies as a public trust; and to appoint to high offices, not the men who wished to use those offices for selfish ends, but men who could do the work best and who took the positions because their services were imperatively needed.

There can be no doubt that this new understanding of the duties of government in our dependencies will have its effect upon our understanding of the duties of government at home. The experience of other nations gives us ground for this belief. When England, at the close of the last century, came to regard India not as a mine to be exploited but as an empire to be administered, the effect did not stop in India. It made its influence felt in the conception of the rights and duties of public officials in England itself. We may expect to see the same result in America—not to be reached in a day or in a year, but by the slow process of educating the public opinion of the next generation. To the boys who are now growing up to manhood, the public approval of the work of men like Taft in the Philippine Islands will be a lesson in political ethics, worth more than a hundred sermons or treatises. It will teach them to apply similar standards in judging what really constitutes political success at home. They will learn that the highest type of honor is not to be obtained by playing a game under certain well defined rules, and abstaining from acts which those rules forbid, but by the subordination of personal convenience and of some of the more obvious forms of personal interest to the needs of public service.

The negative virtue of conforming to the decisions of the courts and abiding by the authority of the law is sufficient for the subjects of a monarchy. It may possibly be sufficient for the members of a democracy where population is so scattered that each man is necessarily occupied in doing nearly everything for his family and relatively little for his neighbors. But when population becomes denser and society more complex, the citizen of a democratic community cannot be content with the mere abstinence from unlawful action. If we would maintain the theory, which is of the very essence of democracy, that every citizen is a gentleman, our citizens must be prepared to accept the responsibilities which go with that claim,—to assume positive duties which they enforce upon themselves without waiting for the control of some outside authority. They must be prepared to subordinate their own personal needs to the needs of the community. When public opinion has frankly accepted this standard of civic duty, then—and not till then—we can have real reform in politics.

The possibilities and the difficulties of political reform are singularly like those of industrial reform. If we condemn a boss when he governs in his interest and in that of his friends, because we would rather govern in our interest and in that of our friends, people will laugh at us. But when we are prepared, so far as opportunity is given us, to use political power in the public interest, at the sacrifice of our own convenience and our own personal advantage, then our condemnation begins to count for something. By the time a large number of sensible men have learned to look at matters in this way, this condemnation will count for everything. It is the voice of such disinterested public opinion, and that alone, which makes the permanent success of democracy possible.

In emergencies America has always enjoyed the benefit of disinterested service from its citizens. In the gravest crises of our national life we have found men like Washington and Lincoln to lead us. Both these men had detractors, who desired to see them removed from power, and organized bitter opposition against them. But it was plain to the great body of freemen that Washington and Lincoln were subordinating individual interest to public duty, and that it was a good thing that men who had this conception of public duty should be placed in office and kept there. It is for us to see that this conception of public office be continuously applied in peace as well as in war. For as the importance of the functions of government increases, the character of the men who administer it from day to day becomes a matter of correspondingly increased importance. We shall be told that we are pursuing impossible ideals; that men's political and industrial actions will necessarily be guided by self-interest; that the conception of politics and industry as games, though it may not be the profoundest or most desirable one, is the only one which we can expect to see realized; and that modification in the rules of the game, by which selfishness shall be turned into less harmful channels, is the best thing that we can expect. We need not be discouraged by these criticisms. Still less need our actions be affected thereby. If these statements are true it means that the days of our democracy are numbered, and that we have before us a fate like that of the Italian republics at the close of the Middle Ages, where wealthy and unscrupulous citizens gained absolute control over the affairs of the state —preserving, indeed, in many instances the forms of a commonwealth, but without either the actual liberty or the actual morality which is essential thereto. But we do not need to look forward to this fate as the probable one. There is every reason to hope that our best men can so influence the community that we shall demand in public affairs the same standards of morality which we voluntarily impose upon ourselves in private ones. We have passed the time when a man's family and personal relations were mere matters of sport. There are, indeed, men who still hold that view; and these are the very ones who are most cynical about the prospects of reform in our industrial or political life. But these men dare not publicly avow those standards of personal morality which would have passed muster a few centuries ago. We have proved the possibility in private life of making the conception of a gentleman's duty at once democratic and Christian—of recognizing his obligations to render sympathy and justice not merely to a few men and women of his own class but to all human beings with whom he comes in contact. It remains for us only to extend this standard of self-imposed obligation so that it shall affect our dealings with masses as well as with separate persons; to be as unwilling to tolerate the oppression of a helpless body of people over whose destinies we have control as we now are to practise cruelty or extortion against those people as individuals; and to demand that our rulers shall recognize these obligations to the public as urgently as we now demand that they shall recognize the obligations of common every-day morality. With this higher standard of industrial and political ethics, a beginning has already been made. In both of these fields we appreciate more fully than our fathers did the importance of political and industrial trusts, and the wide range of duties which the acceptance of such trusts carries with it. If we will use our utmost endeavors to see straight, to think clearly, and to govern ourselves by the same standards which we seek to impose upon others, we can look forward with confidence to the perpetuation of personal liberty, and to the permanence of democratic institutions.

INDEX

ANARCHISTS, toleration of, 97, 98
Arbitration, 137-139
Aristotle's political theories, 2, 146
Atonement, conception of, 59, 60

BAGEHOT, Physics and Politics, 53, 54, 99

CARLYLE on Liberty, 98
Checks and balances, effect of, 17, 18
Civil remedies, 77, 78
Coal combinations, 134-140
Combinations, management of, 133-136
Commercial standards of morals, 145, 146
Competition, 119-123, 158; difficulties of, 128-136; in politics, 164
Congress, change in functions of, 14-16
Consciousness, 49, 57, 58
Conspiracy, 139-142

Contract, system of, 75, 78-81, 136-139
Constitution of the United States, 10-18
Constitutional limitation, character of, 30
Corporation law and ethics, 81, 82, 157-160

DEBATE in legislative bodies, 13-15
Directors, duties of, 159, 160

ECONOMIC freedom, 116-120
Egoism, rational, 107-110
Emancipation, 46; mediæval, 112-115
English constitutional theory, 29; political morality, 167, 168
Ethics, origin of, 50-54
Evolution, in man and in the lower animals, 50-52
Expiation, 59

FREEDOM of teaching, 95-98; of the will, 48-72
French Revolution, 5-7

INDEX

GOVERNMENT management of industry, 142–144

ILLEGITIMATE government, 2
Individualism, 102; limits of, 126–144
Industrial morality, modern, 155–157
Insanity, conception of, 87–89
Instinct, 49–51
Interest, ethics of, 116

JEVONS on combination, 140
Judiciary, American, 23, 24

LAISSEZ faire, 105
Lassalle, 128
Law, evolution of, 63, 64; separated from morals, 61
Legitimate government, 2

MARSHALL, H. R., on religious observance, 56
Mediæval economic changes, 112–115
Merit, 69
Mill on Liberty, 83, 84
Morality, ancient, 64, 65; modern, 153–155
Morley, doctrine of liberty, 98, 99, 104

NEGRO suffrage, 39–43
Nullification, 37

PARLIAMENTARY government, 9
Party machinery in the United States, 18–23
Passive resistance, 37
Personal responsibility, 62
Political ethics, modern, 161–164
Populism, 2–7
Precedent, authority of, 33, 34
Private judgment, 46
Prophets, work of, 87–89

RELIGION, origin of, 53–58
Religious observance, 55, 56, 85, 86
Remedies, civil and criminal, 77, 78
Responsibility, personal, 62
Reversion, 52
Roman law of contracts, 78, 79
Rousseau on sovereignty, 5, 35

SACRIFICE, 59, 60
Self-regarding acts, 84, 85
Self-restraint the basis of liberty, 25, 27, 45
Socialism, 142–146
Sovereignty, theory of, 34, 35
Status, system of, 74–77

TEACHING, freedom of, 95–98
Toleration, 58, 87, 102, 103

Trusts, ethical aspect of, 157–160; political, 166–168

USURY, 116

VALUE, ethical theory of, 117–120

WARRANTY, 81
Will, freedom of, 48–72